ONE-BEER GRILLING

ONE-BEER
GRILLING

FAST, EASY & FRESH FORMULAS
FOR GREAT GRILLED MEALS YOU CAN MAKE
BEFORE YOU FINISH YOUR FIRST COLD ONE

MIKE LANG

CASTLE POINT BOOKS
NEW YORK

TO MOM & DAD—
FOR JUST BEING YOU AND FOR ALWAYS BEING THERE.

⸺ CONTENTS ⸺

—INTRODUCTION—

Welcome to *One-Beer Grilling*. The fact you that are reading this tells me we already have a lot in common. Whenever I fire up a grill, a beer is guaranteed to be close by—if not in a recipe, then definitely in my hand. I trust you are the same.

I've dedicated breakfasts, lunches, and more dinners than I can count to perfecting the art of grilling. It's a process of trial and error, exploration, and, coincidentally, a time to enjoy a lot of great beer. As documented through the writing and photography on my blog, *Another Pint Please*, and on the pages of *Sports Illustrated*, and, most proudly, in the global reach of the world's largest grill manufacturer, Weber Grills, my love for live-fire cooking and beer has only grown. I'm excited to hit the pause button on my journey and share with you my grilling exploits and adventures.

Honed from years of grilling food on the twenty grills in my backyard, the recipes in this collection add new twists to classics and make those that may seem challenging to grill more approachable. Some recipes, like my Red Pepper Bites or Carolina Pork Sliders, take about one beer to grill. But others, such as the Smoked Prime Rib or Pulled Pork, take hours, leaving the beer for the final feast. And some, like Smoked Pork Chili or Beer-Can Chicken, include one beer in the recipe. That one beer, no matter how or where we enjoy it, is essential.

Before you pour your first cold one, here are a few things to consider:

★ TYPES OF GRILLS

There are an astounding number of grills on the market and a wide variety of fuel sources. Whether you own a gas grill, a charcoal grill, a smoker, a kamado grill, or a pellet grill, you will be able to adapt these recipes to your cooker type and make a fantastic grilled dinner.

Recipes are cooked over either direct heat or indirect heat. Direct heat means the heating source is directly under the food. For instance, on a gas grill, all of the burners would be on. On a charcoal grill, the food would be directly over lit briquettes on the grate. You will often see this method called for when cooking food for a relatively short amount of time. Indirect heat means the food is not directly over the heat source. On a three-burner gas grill, picture the middle burner turned off, with the food directly above it. On a charcoal grill, the briquettes are pushed to one side of the grill, creating a two-zone fire with direct heat on one side and indirect heat on the other. Understanding and controlling the grill's heat are the keys to success.

★ TIME AND TEMPERATURE

No, I'm not talking about the days when you could grab your rotary phone and dial the operator for the time and weather. Knowing the target internal-cook temperature and the approximate amount of time it takes to get there is crucial for grilling a successful meal. Whenever beer is involved, there is a high probability of getting off track! So use a kitchen timer to keep you on track and in tune. The timer has your back and has saved me more than once. An instant-read thermometer is for the last lap. A perfectly cooked steak, chop, or roast can go from fantastic to failure in just a matter of degrees. A good thermometer is a must.

★ PLANKING

While planking might be a feat of strength, I use it here as another way to add flavor to food on the grill. Cooking on cedar planks dates back hundreds of years and is just as relevant and approachable today. For many, and rightfully so, planking immediately conjures an image of Cedar Plank Salmon. It's not uncommon to see salmon served this way, even in a restaurant. However, planking is hardly limited to seafood. This book has recipes for planking appetizers, beef, chicken, and even mashed potatoes. When planking, be sure to use food-safe grilling planks, and if you are unable to locate the different wood varieties I list, just use cedar planks, which are readily available at most grocery and hardware stores. Planks are a great way of improving your grilling game and impressing your guests.

If you have made it this far, not only do I know we have similar interests, but we could be close friends. My neighbors see me in front of a grill in the summer's heat and in the cold, snowy nights of winter. It is part passion and part pursuit of the perfectly grilled meal. I've met a lot of folks who see their grills as one-trick ponies, à la burgers on the weekend. The desire is there to grill more, but it is often hard to stray from what's known. No matter what type of grill you own, my goal is to broaden your grilling horizons. I hardly know it all, but the techniques I share in *One-Beer Grilling* will give you the confidence and know-how to make unforgettable feasts for family and friends. They have worked for me, and I hope they will for you, too.

Grilling, like life, is a process of continuous improvement. Whenever I'm over a live fire, there is the potential to learn a new trick or spark a crazy idea. I hope you will join me on this journey. Now let's grab a beer and fire up the grill.

CHAPTER 1

APPETIZERS

GRILLED
EGGPLANT CAPRESE

★ **SERVES 4**

★ **INGREDIENTS**

2 large tomatoes,
cut into ¼-inch slices

1 large eggplant,
cut into ¼-inch slices

1 pound mozzarella cheese,
cut into ¼-inch slices

1 tablespoon kosher salt

Olive oil

12 fresh basil leaves

Store-bought balsamic glaze

★ **BEER PAIRING**
Berliner Weisse

The grill is fantastic for changing the flavor profile of foods that you wouldn't always think to grill. Caprese salads are usually served cold with the freshest of ingredients. As someone who was never a big raw tomato fan growing up, I have passed on more capreses than I have consumed. This all changed one day when I decided to grill one. Grilling a tomato slice, one of the salad's bases, can be tricky, but with a clean grill, the right temperature, and good timing, it's easy. Adding in slices of meaty grilled eggplant nearly pushes this appetizer into dinner territory. And those grilled tomatoes? They're sweet and delicious.

1 Prepare a grill for direct medium heat (350° to 450°F).

2 Brush both sides of the tomato and eggplant slices with olive oil and season them with salt.

3 Grill the tomatoes and eggplant slices over direct heat until they are marked, flipping once, 3 to 4 minutes per side.

4 Place an eggplant slice on a plate. Top it with a slice of mozzarella, a basil leaf, and a slice of tomato. Repeat. Finish with a drizzle of balsamic glaze.

PLANKED
PORTOBELLOS

My mom will be proud; I've included lots of vegetables in this book. When I was younger, I wasn't very fond of a lot of these foods. Culinarily speaking, my upbringing was decidedly midwestern, and in the center lane. Sure, my folks took some interesting exits growing up, but the late '70s and early '80s were not exactly a high point in the suburban kitchen. On the list of foods I often skipped over were mushrooms. Granted, I use the ingredient "mushroom" to account for every type of mushroom. Perhaps if I had discovered portobellos sooner, my outlook would have changed. These meaty beasts are great for holding cheese and for taking on the aroma of a smoldering cedar plank. It's a wonderful appetizer that I'm pretty sure younger me would have enjoyed.

★ **SERVES 4**

★ **INGREDIENTS**
1 tablespoon pine nuts
2 portobello mushroom caps
8 ounces feta cheese
4 cloves garlic, minced
¼ cup chopped fresh basil

★ **EQUIPMENT**
Cedar grilling plank,
soaked in water for 30 minutes

★ **BEER PAIRING**
English Mild

1 In a skillet over medium heat, toast the pine nuts until fragrant, 2 to 3 minutes.

2 Prepare a grill for direct medium heat (350° to 450°F).

3 In a small bowl, combine the feta, garlic, and basil.

4 Rinse the mushrooms and remove any dirt. With a spoon, scrape out the gills and discard.

5 Grill one side of the plank over direct medium heat until the plank starts to smolder, about 1 to 2 minutes.

6 Place the mushrooms on the burned side of the plank. Fill the mushroom caps equally with the cheese mixture and top with the pine nuts.

7 Grill the plank over direct medium heat until the cheese begins to brown, about 7 to 10 minutes.

GRILLED NACHOS

★ **SERVES 4**

★ **INGREDIENTS**
Tortilla chips

8 ounces shredded Monterey Jack cheese

8 ounces shredded cheddar cheese

½ cup quartered cherry tomatoes

½ cup black beans, drained and rinsed

1 jalapeño pepper, sliced

¼ cup sour cream

¼ cup store-bought salsa

★ **EQUIPMENT**
Cast-iron skillet or perforated grill pan

★ **BEER PAIRING**
German Pilsner

I've never met a pile of nachos I didn't like. In fact, it's one of my favorite things to make, and depending on my mood, it can take on any number of proteins and toppings. Nachos are versatile, delicious, and simply amazing on the grill. This recipe for grilled nachos is an excellent example of using grill accessories. When using a cast-iron skillet or perforated grill pan, all of the ingredients are contained within it, making nachos, no matter the toppings, incredibly easy to grill. And speaking of toppings, with nachos, anything is possible. Below I give you the basic recipe for my favorite late-day snack. For more flare, consider topping with shredded chicken and mozzarella cheese or grilled skirt steak and queso, or my favorite, beefy chili and sharp cheddar cheese. Once you have the process down, use your favorite toppings to make these nachos your own.

1 Prepare a grill for indirect medium heat (350° to 450°F).

2 Arrange a layer of tortilla chips in the bottom of a cast-iron skillet.

3 Top with cheese, tomatoes, and black beans. Add another layer of tortilla chips and repeat. Continue until the layers rise out of the skillet. Top with jalapeño slices.

4 Grill the nachos over indirect heat until the cheese melts, approximately 10 to 15 minutes.

5 In a small bowl, combine the sour cream and salsa. Top the nachos with the mixture and serve.

SMOKED
BEER CHEESE

★ **INGREDIENTS**

3 tablespoons flour

3 tablespoons unsalted butter

½ cup whole milk

1 cup amber lager

½ shallot, minced

1 teaspoon Worcestershire sauce

1 teaspoon Dijon mustard

1 cup shredded Gouda cheese

½ cup shredded cheddar cheese

½ cup shredded mozzarella cheese

1 teaspoon diced green chilis

Crusty bread or tortilla chips

★ **EQUIPMENT**

8-inch cast-iron skillet

Hickory wood chunk or chips

★ **BEER PAIRING**

Smoked Porter

As far as I am concerned, beer and cheese are their own food groups. Beer cheese is a great example of my grilling adage, "take it outside." While the stovetop is needed to start this recipe, all the action happens on the grill. Taking meals outside allows me to turn things upside down, introducing new flavors and elements that just aren't possible in the kitchen. It makes good meals better and always more interesting. Sure, beer cheese is good. Smoked beer cheese? Hold my chips...and my beer.

1 Heat an 8-inch cast-iron skillet on the stove top over medium-low heat. Melt the butter and whisk in the flour until combined and fragrant, approximately 1 minute.

2 Add the milk, and continue to whisk for 1 minute. Add the lager. While still whisking, raise the heat to medium-high and cook until the contents begin to boil and thicken, approximately 2 minutes.

3 Stir in the shallots, Worcestershire sauce, and mustard.

4 Stir in the cheese until melted. Top with the chilis.

5 Prepare the grill for indirect medium-low heat (200° to 250°F). Once at temperature, add a hickory wood chunk to the lit briquettes or, on a gas grill, add hickory wood chips to a smoker box or foil packet.

6 Grill the cheese-filled skillet over indirect heat for approximately 30 minutes, stirring occasionally.

7 Remove and serve with crusty bread or tortilla chips.

PLANKED
SHRIMP COCKTAIL

Growing up, I was a shrimp cocktail fiend. Whenever my parents took my siblings and me to a restaurant where shrimp cocktail was on the menu, it only took a knowing glance from my dad to know it was going down. The only debate was how many shrimp I had to share with my brothers and sister. As the eldest, I always tried to claim more. I mean, who wouldn't? I never really thought of shrimp cocktail—an appetizer served cold—as a "cooked food," but it most certainly is. Cooking the shrimp on a wooden plank placed directly on top of the coals adds an abundance of flavor beyond the typical boiled shrimp. It's a hot and fast cook, and when done, with the shrimp nicely chilled, it's a shrimp cocktail my dad would have rightly kept for himself.

★ **SERVES 2**

★ **INGREDIENTS**
10 shrimp, extra-large (raw, deveined, tail on)
2 cups water
2 tablespoons kosher salt
1 lemon, quartered, divided
Cocktail sauce

★ **EQUIPMENT**
Cedar grilling plank, soaked in water for an hour prior to grilling
2 one-gallon resealable plastic bags

★ **BEER PAIRING**
Amber Ale

1 For the brine: In a saucepan on a stovetop, bring the water to a boil. Add two lemon quarters and stir in the salt until it dissolves. Remove the pan from the heat and allow it to cool, then refrigerate it until it's cold.

2 Add the shrimp and the chilled brine to a plastic bag. Seal and refrigerate it for 1 to 2 hours.

3 In a charcoal grill, arrange the briquettes in a single layer. The briquettes will appear light gray and ashed over when ready.

4 Remove the shrimp from the brine and discard the brine and the bag.

5 Place the shrimp on the soaked plank and place the remaining lemon quarters on the shrimp.

6 Place the plank directly on the coals and lower the lid. Grill until the shrimp turn opaque, approximately 6 to 8 minutes.

7 Place the cooked shrimp and lemon quarters in a clean bag. Remove the air and seal. Chill the bag of shrimp in a large bowl of ice water. Remove the shrimp and lemon from the bag and serve with cocktail sauce.

PLANKED BRIE

When I am entertaining family or friends, Planked Brie is almost always on the menu. A French cow's milk cheese, Brie can be sliced and enjoyed cold, but it transforms into something amazing when grilled on a plank. Grilling cheese might seem like a crazy idea, but Brie is perfectly suited for it. The white rind contains the cheese as it goes from soft to gooey. A smoldering plank adds a wonderful layer of smokiness to the cheese and performs double-duty as a serving platter. Once it's off the grill and sliced open, the Brie oozes onto the board, only to be eagerly scooped up with crackers or chips. It's easy to see why it's always a hit.

---

1 Prepare a grill for indirect medium heat (350° to 450°F).

2 Grill one side of the plank over direct medium heat until the plank starts to smolder, about 1 to 2 minutes.

3 Remove the Brie from the paper wrapper and place it on the burned side of the plank.

4 Top the Brie with the preserves and almonds.

5 Grill the plank over indirect heat until the cheese becomes soft and browned, approximately 10 to 15 minutes.

6 Serve with crackers or chips.

★ **SERVES 4**

★ **INGREDIENTS**
8-ounce Brie wheel
2 tablespoons strawberry preserves
1 tablespoon sliced almonds
Crackers or chips

★ **EQUIPMENT**
Cedar grilling plank,
soaked in water for 30 minutes

★ **BEER PAIRING**
Belgian Blonde Ale

BACON-WRAPPED
PINEAPPLE SKEWERS

★ **SERVES 4**

★ **INGREDIENTS**

16 pineapple chunks,
about 1-inch square

8 slices bacon

½ teaspoon cayenne pepper

★ **EQUIPMENT**

4 wooden skewers,
soaked in water for 30 minutes

★ **BEER PAIRING**

Kolsch

At first glance, fruit might seem unusual to grill, but its subtle sweetness is a perfect complement to a hot grate. When I'm staring at brimming baskets of freshly picked strawberries and raspberries, I'm already thinking of how many skewers I'm going to need to load up my grill. If I haven't sold you on grilling fruit yet, let's dip our tongs in the water with a mixture of sweet, savory, and spicy loaded skewers. Pineapple, in particular, is a terrific fruit to grill, creating sweet caramelization as the fruit takes on heat. A dash of cayenne keeps things popping, and the bacon is a perfect savory balance to the pineapple's tropical sweetness.

1   Wrap each pineapple chunk with half a slice of bacon. Slide the bacon-wrapped pineapple onto a skewer. Each skewer should hold 4 chunks, with space between each piece.

2   Season the bacon-wrapped fruit evenly with cayenne.

3   Prepare a grill for indirect medium heat (350° to 450°F).

4   Grill the pineapple-loaded skewers over indirect heat until the bacon renders and the pineapple is heated through, approximately 25 to 30 minutes. Remove from the skewers and serve.

RED PEPPER BITES

If there is a constant refrain in my life, it is "less is more." (A close second is, "pick up sticks in the lawn before mowing," but the former wins out.) Often the simplest and easiest foods to hit the grill are "less," but also incredible. Enter these Red Pepper Bites, a snackable flavor bomb to enjoy with beer while the main course is smoking away. Not only do these treats cover three of the original four food groups, but they are also a one-handed appetizer. No sooner do I pull these babies off the grill than my friends will start grabbing them off the platter and tossing them into their mouths as they head for their next beer. Simple to prepare; easy to grill; so good you will want to come back for more.

★ **SERVES 10**

★ **INGREDIENTS**

3 red bell peppers

1 pound ground chuck (80/20)

1 pound pork sausage

¼ cup panko bread crumbs

1 teaspoon kosher salt

1 teaspoon granulated garlic

½ teaspoon freshly cracked black pepper

6 ounces cheddar cheese, cut into 1-inch slices

★ **BEER PAIRING**

English Brown Ale

1 Slice the red pepper into planks, then cut them into approximately 1-inch squares.

2 In a large bowl, combine the ground chuck, sausage, bread crumbs, salt, garlic, and black pepper.

3 Prepare a grill for indirect medium heat (350° to 450°F).

4 Place a spoonful of the meat mixture onto each red pepper square.

5 Grill the pepper bites over indirect medium heat until the meat reads 155°F with an instant-read thermometer, approximately 15 to 20 minutes. Top with a slice of cheddar cheese during the last 5 minutes of cooking.

SMOKED
JALAPEÑO POPPERS

★ **SERVES 3**

★ **INGREDIENTS**

6 jalapeño peppers

12 ounces cream cheese

½ cup cheddar cheese, grated

3 tablespoons store-bought BBQ rub, divided

6 slices bacon

¼ cup Parmigiano-Reggiano cheese, grated

★ **EQUIPMENT**

Hickory wood chunks or chips

★ **BEER PAIRING**

German Dunkel

I've eaten my fair share of fried jalapeño poppers at restaurants and bars. I've also burned the roof of my mouth on them more times than I can count. For as great as they can be, they are so much better when smoked low and slow on a grill versus taking a plunge in a vat of hot cooking oil. The spice level with my poppers is subtle, yet flavorful. The best part is the salty balance of smoked bacon to spicy cheese. Every bite will have you anticipating the next, and better yet, the roof of your mouth will be safe. Grab a beer and your grill and kiss those deep-fried poppers good bye.

1 Slice the jalapeños in half lengthwise. With a spoon, scoop out and discard the ribs and seeds.

2 In a small bowl, mix together the cream cheese, cheddar cheese and 2 tablespoons of your favorite BBQ rub.

3 Fill the jalapeño halves with the cream cheese mixture.

4 Sprinkle the filled jalapeños with the remaining rub and top with the freshly grated cheese.

5 Slice the bacon strips in half lengthwise and then wrap a bacon strip around each popper.

6 Prepare the grill for indirect low heat (200° to 250°F). Once at temperature, add the hickory wood chunk to the lit briquettes or, on a gas grill, add hickory wood chips to a smoker box or foil packet.

7 Place the poppers on the grill, lower the lid, and smoke for approximately 40 to 50 minutes or until the bacon has rendered and the cheese is heated through.

GRILLED
STUFFED AVOCADOS

Avocados are probably not the first grill-friendly food you think of, but they taste amazing when cooked over a live fire. They are also fantastic when they act as a vessel for more food, in this case a medley of onions, peppers, bacon, and cheese. While you can mark the soft avocado flesh on the grate, the more resilient shell is perfectly suited to endure prolonged periods over direct heat. The heat allows the fruit to soften, the toppings to meld, and the cheese to melt. This recipe can also easily become vegetarian by removing the bacon. And my favorite variation? Add a fried egg and suddenly you've turned an appetizer into breakfast.

1 On the stovetop, in a small skillet over low heat, add the butter and olive oil. Once the butter has melted, add the onion and green pepper. Cook for approximately 20 to 25 minutes, stirring periodically.

2 In another skillet over medium heat, cook the bacon until it's just crispy and the fat has rendered, approximately 8 to 10 minutes. Place the bacon on paper towels to soak up the fat, then chop the bacon.

3 Slice the avocados in half and remove the pit.

4 Combine the cumin, salt, and black pepper and use the mixture to season the avocado flesh.

5 Divide the onion and pepper mixture among the avocado halves, filling up the hole left by the pit.

6 Top each avocado with bacon.

7 Prepare a grill for direct medium heat (350° to 450°F).

8 Grill the avocados, skin side down, over direct heat until they are soft when gently squeezed, approximately 20 to 25 minutes. Add the cheese during the last 5 minutes of cooking.

★ **SERVES 4**

★ **INGREDIENTS**
1 tablespoon unsalted butter
1 tablespoon extra-virgin olive oil
1 small sweet onion, sliced
1 small green bell pepper, sliced
2 avocados, slightly soft to the touch
1 teaspoon cumin
½ teaspoon kosher salt
¼ teaspoon freshly cracked black pepper
2 slices bacon
4 ¼-inch slices extra-sharp cheddar cheese

★ **BEER PAIRING**
Vienna Lager

CHAPTER 2

RED MEAT

CHIPOTLE-MARINATED
SKIRT STEAK TACOS

★ **SERVES 4**

★ **INGREDIENTS**

1 ½ to 2 pounds skirt steak

1 7-ounce can chipotles in adobo sauce, pureed

3 green onions, chopped, divided

2 limes, divided

6 cilantro sprigs, divided

Extra-virgin olive oil

1 teaspoon kosher salt

8 flour tortillas

½ cup shredded cheddar cheese

½ cup shredded Monterey jack cheese

Store-bought salsa

★ **EQUIPMENT**

One-gallon resealable plastic bag

Aluminum foil

★ **BEER PAIRING**

Dortmunder

There may be Taco Tuesday, but I subscribe to Taco Any-day. The tortilla can be the vehicle for anything, so having tacos any day, let alone every day, isn't really a stretch. This is one of my favorite recipes. Skirt steak can be a tough cut of meat, but when cooked hot and fast and cut into small pieces, it is incredibly meaty and tender. Contrary to popular belief, a marinade does not tenderize meat, but it does add flavor, which is later locked in by the hot searing action of the grill. Fresh toppings for tacos are a must, but no matter what you add, be sure to finish them off with freshly squeezed lime juice. The lime's citrus tang is the ultimate finishing touch.

1 Remove any excess fat from the skirt steak.

2 In a resealable plastic bag, add the pureed chipotles, two-thirds of the chopped green onions, the garlic, the juice of one lime, and 3 cilantro sprigs. Add the steak.

3 Remove all of the air from the bag and allow the steak to marinate in the refrigerator for 4 to 6 hours. Rotate the bag every couple of hours.

4 Prepare a grill for direct high heat (450° to 550°F).

5 Remove the steak from the bag and pat it dry. Discard the marinade.

6 Lightly brush the steak with olive oil and season it with kosher salt.

7 Grill the steak over direct high heat for 5 to 6 minutes, flipping once. For medium-rare, cook until the internal temperature reads 135°F with an instant-read thermometer.

8 Transfer the steak to a cutting board, tent with aluminum foil, and allow it to rest.

9 Place the tortillas in aluminum foil and warm them on the grill for 1 to 2 minutes over indirect heat.

10 Cut the steak into ½-inch pieces.

11 To serve, load each tortilla with steak, remaining green onions, cilantro, a spritz of lime juice, cheese, and salsa.

CHEESY BEER
PIT-BEEF SANDWICHES

If you have ever spent time in Baltimore, Maryland, you know what pit beef is. For the uninitiated, this Charm City creation is a top or bottom round roast, grilled medium-rare, sliced thin, and served with onions on a roll. The star here is the bottom round roast. This cut is relatively inexpensive and, when highly seasoned and properly cooked, incredibly delicious. A sharp knife can work wonders, but if you have access to a meat slicer, this is the cut to use it on: the thinner the slices, the more tender the meat. It's one of my favorites.

1   With a sharp knife, remove any excess fat or silver skin from the roast.

2   In a small bowl, combine the rub ingredients. Evenly season the roast with the rub. Truss the roast with butcher twine.

3   Prepare the grill for indirect low heat (200° to 250°F).

4   Grill the roast over low heat until the internal temperature reads 115°F with an instant-read thermometer, approximately 60 to 75 minutes.

5   Remove the roast from the grill, tent with aluminum foil, and allow it to rest.

6   To make the cheese sauce, melt the butter in a small saucepan over medium heat. Add the flour to the butter and whisk constantly until combined and fragrant, about 1 minute.

7   Raise the temperature of the saucepan to medium-high and slowly add the milk, then the beer, while whisking. Continue to whisk until the sauce thickens and coats the back of a spoon, about 4 to 5 minutes. Season with salt and pepper.

8   Reduce the heat to low. Stir in the cheddar cheese until the cheese melts. Keep warm over low heat.

9   Prepare the grill for direct high heat (450° to 550°F). Grill the roast over direct heat for 4 minutes, 1 minute each side. Grill the buns cut side down over direct heat until marked, about 1 minute.

10 Thinly slice the roast. Place the sliced beef on a bun, top with the cheese sauce, a pickled jalapeño, and the top of the bun. Serve.

★ **SERVES 4**

★ **INGREDIENTS**
3 to 5 pounds bottom round roast

FOR THE RUB
1 teaspoon granulated garlic
1 teaspoon dried rosemary
1 teaspoon kosher salt
1 teaspoon freshly cracked black pepper

FOR THE CHEESE SAUCE
3 tablespoons butter
3 tablespoons all-purpose flour
1 cup milk
½ cup stout beer
¼ teaspoon kosher salt
⅛ teaspoon freshly cracked black pepper
3 cups shredded cheddar cheese

4 pretzel buns
4 pickled jalapeños

★ **EQUIPMENT**
Butcher twine
Aluminum foil

★ **BEER PAIRING**
American Pale Ale

PLANKED MEATBALLS

★ **SERVES 3**

★ **INGREDIENTS**

12 meatballs
(store-bought or homemade)

½ teaspoon kosher salt

½ teaspoon freshly cracked
black pepper

½ cup marinara sauce
(store-bought or homemade)

⅓ cup grated Parmigiano-Reggiano
cheese

★ **EQUIPMENT**

Oak grilling plank, soaked in water
for 30 minutes

★ **BEER PAIRING**

American Stout

This is what happens when I leave the house thinking of my grilling planks and then find fresh meatballs at the grocery store. Enter, planked meatballs. Planking the meatballs saves time, and the smoldering board is a fantastic "flavor blanket" that coats the meatballs in its sweet smoke. I present the concept here, which is incredibly easy with quality store-bought products, and even better if you make your own meatballs and sauce. But if you are pressed for time and still want to see those coals catch fire, this is the last-minute meal for you.

1   Prepare the grill with a two-zone fire for both direct and indirect medium heat (350° to 450°F).

2   Grill one side of the plank over direct medium heat until the plank starts to smolder, about 1 to 2 minutes.

3   Place the meatballs on the plank and season them with salt and pepper. Place the plank over direct heat and grill, with the lid closed, for 15 minutes.

4   Slide the plank to indirect heat. Top the meatballs with marinara sauce. Lower the lid and grill an additional 10 minutes.

5   Top the meatballs with the grated cheese.

6   Grill until the internal temperature of the meatballs reaches 160°F with an instant-read thermometer, approximately 3 to 5 minutes.

SMOKED PRIME RIB

One of my favorite meals for entertaining is prime rib. It has it all: well-seasoned, succulent meat, beautiful presentation, and there is always plenty to go around. A standing rib roast can be grilled as is. However, for that "wow factor" presentation, consider removing the meat around the bones, otherwise known as "frenching." While this is not difficult to execute, it's even easier to ask your butcher to do it. While the word "prime" evokes the grade of cut, in this case "prime rib" refers to the type of cut as one of the eight primal cuts of meat. These eight primal cuts are the sections first removed during butchering. So if I pick up a three-bone standing rib roast graded as Choice, the USDA says I can still call it prime rib even though it's not technically USDA Prime. In the end, call it what you want.
I call it "awesome."

---

1 Prepare a grill for indirect medium-low heat (250° to 300°F).

2 Combine the rub ingredients in a small bowl and then evenly cover the roast with the rub.

3 Truss the roast by wrapping a piece of butcher twine around the meat and securing it tightly next to a bone. Repeat for each bone of the roast.

4 Once at temperature, add an oak wood chunk to lit briquettes or, on a gas grill, add oak wood chips to a smoker box or foil packet.

5 Grill over indirect heat for approximately 1½ to 2 hours, or until the internal temperature of the roast reads 125°F on an instant-read thermometer.

6 Remove from the grill, tent with foil, and allow the meat to rest 15 to 20 minutes.

7 Separate the bones, then slice and serve.

★ **SERVES 6**

★ **INGREDIENTS**
Bone-in standing rib roast
(3 bone, 7 to 9 pounds), frenched

FOR THE RUB
2 tablespoons kosher salt
1 tablespoon black pepper
1 tablespoon granulated garlic
1 teaspoon onion powder

★ **EQUIPMENT**
Butcher twine
Oak wood chunk or chips
Aluminum foil

★ **BEER PAIRING**
Baltic Porter

REVERSE-SEAR
TOMAHAWK STEAK

★ **SERVES 2**

★ **INGREDIENTS**

1 tomahawk rib-eye steak, approximately 2½ pounds

1 teaspoon extra-virgin olive oil

1 teaspoon kosher salt

1 teaspoon freshly cracked black pepper

½ teaspoon garlic powder

★ **EQUIPMENT**

Aluminum foil

★ **BEER PAIRING**

Barrel-Aged Porter

Grilling meat that's more than 1½ inches thick to a perfect medium-rare can be a challenge. To get the center cooked to the proper doneness, the outer edges of the meat take on more heat, cooking them well past the target temperature. To achieve the elusive "wall to wall" pink of a perfectly cooked steak, I use a combination of indirect and direct heat in a process known as the reverse sear. Slowly grilling the meat over indirect low heat to a temperature just short of medium-rare brings the internal temperature up evenly. After a short rest, finish the steak with a hot and fast sear to create an unforgettable crust. Yielding a perfectly cooked middle with a flavorful crust, the reverse sear is a go-to tool in my grilling "toolbox."

1 Brush the steak with olive oil and season all over with salt, pepper, and garlic powder. Don't forget to season the sides of the steak.

2 Prepare a grill for indirect low heat (200° to 250°F).

3 For medium-rare, grill the steak over indirect low heat until the internal temperature reads 115°F with an instant-read thermometer, approximately 45 to 60 minutes.

4 Remove the steak from the grill. Tent the meat with aluminum foil and allow it to rest at least 15 minutes.

5 Prepare a grill for direct high heat (450° to 550°F).

6 Grill the steak over direct high heat for 2 minutes, flipping once.

7 Remove the steak from the grill, slice, and serve.

GRILLED CHEESE AND
STEAK SANDWICHES

Grilled cheese sandwiches are one of those childhood comfort foods I often find myself seeking out. Whether I plan ahead or I'm simply trying to find a way to empty the contents of the fridge, there is nothing quite like griddle-fried bread and soft melted cheese to please the palate. My grilled cheese sandwiches have matured over the years. White bread and American cheese have taken a backseat to artisanal loaves and funky cheeses. In this sandwich riff, I add chopped steak and one other twist unavailable to me at age eight, the grill. It packs just a little extra smoky love the stovetop cannot.

1   Prepare the grill for direct medium heat (350° to 450°F). Preheat the cast-iron skillet over direct heat.

2   Spread mayonnaise on all 4 slices of bread and place the bread, mayonnaise side down, on a cutting board.

3   Spread Dijon mustard on two slices of the bread. Evenly top each Dijon slice with the cheeses and steak and add a few dashes of your favorite hot sauce.

4   Top the sandwiches with the remaining slice of bread so the mayonnaise side faces up.

5   Using the cast-iron skillet, grill the sandwiches over direct heat until the bread has browned and the cheese had melted, approximately 8 minutes, flipping once.

★ **SERVES 2**

★ **INGREDIENTS**
   4 slices farmhouse white bread
   2 tablespoons mayonnaise
   2 teaspoons Dijon mustard
   1 cup shredded cheddar cheese
   1 cup shredded fontina cheese
   ½ cup cooked, chopped steak
   Hot sauce

★ **EQUIPMENT**
   Cast-iron skillet

★ **BEER PAIRING**
   American Pale Ale

STUFFED FLANK STEAK
WITH PROSCIUTTO AND GOAT CHEESE

★ **SERVES 4**

★ **INGREDIENTS**
1 flank steak, 3 to 4 pounds
5 slices prosciutto
½ cup chopped walnuts
½ cup fresh flat-leaf parsley
1 clove garlic, minced
4 ounces goat cheese
Kosher salt and black pepper
Extra-virgin olive oil

★ **EQUIPMENT**
Butcher twine

★ **BEER PAIRING**
Imperial Stout

Flank steak is a cut that is sometimes overlooked, which is a shame, because it has so much going for it. Flank is a leaner, less tender cut than a strip steak or rib-eye, and cooking it to a proper temperature and then slicing across the grain is key. To ensure consistent success while packing in even more flavor and texture, I love to butterfly it, stuff it, and roll it. The trickiest part is the butterfly. A sharp knife and a steady hand are essential to split the steak in half without cutting through.

1   Remove any excess fat and silver skin from the flank steak.

2   Butterfly the flank steak: Start at one corner of a long edge and cut into the center of the steak. Keep the knife parallel to the work surface and until the meat can open like a book. Flip the steak over. The flank steak should be of uniform thickness. If any meat is remaining at the "spine," remove it. Flip the steak back over so the muscle fibers run from left to right.

3   Season the meat generously with salt and pepper.

4   Starting at the closest edge, line the steak with prosciutto slices.

5   In a small food processor, grind the walnuts, parsley, and garlic. Spread the mixture evenly across the prosciutto, keeping it several inches away from the far long edge. Add the goat cheese the same way.

6   Keeping the meat tight, roll the steak away from you toward the far edge.

7   Using butcher twine, secure the flank steak by starting in the middle of the steak with the first piece of twine and working with additional pieces of twine toward the outside. Five knots should easily hold the steak together.

8   Prepare the grill for direct and indirect medium-high heat (400° to 450°F).

9   Lightly brush the steak with olive oil.

10 Sear each side of the steak over direct heat for approximately 2 minutes a side, 8 minutes total. Move the steak to indirect heat and continue to grill until the internal temperature is 130°F with an instant-read thermometer, approximately 20 minutes.

11 Slice into half-inch pieces and serve.

HAWAIIAN BURGERS

I realize that, to some, the idea of adding fruit to a hamburger is unsettling. We probably all have a "secret" combination of foods that we love but that others find reprehensible. I've heard the "no anchovies on my pizza" line more times than I can count, and every time I do, I think of the wonderful anchovy salt bombs those naysayers are missing. So as I try to coax you into this meat-and-fruit combo, I recognize that it might take some convincing. However, one bite of this flavor bomb burger is all you will need to become a true believer. The bold beef flavor of the patty is accentuated by the saltiness of the teriyaki and balanced by the sweetness of the grilled pineapple. Each bite will keep you coming back for more. It's different. It's delicious.

★ **SERVES 4**

★ **INGREDIENTS**
2 pounds ground chuck (80/20)
¾ teaspoon kosher salt
½ teaspoon garlic powder
¼ teaspoon freshly cracked black pepper
4 pineapple slices
⅓ cup store-bought teriyaki glaze
4 slices mozzarella cheese
4 hamburger buns

★ **BEER PAIRING**
California Common

1. In a medium bowl, mix together the ground chuck, kosher salt, garlic powder, and black pepper.

2. Divide the mixture into 4 equal-size balls and then press into patties. With your thumb, leave an indentation in the bottom of each patty. This keeps the patty from swelling when on the grill.

3. Prepare a grill for direct medium-high heat, 400° to 500°F.

4. Grill the pineapple slices over direct heat for 2 minutes, flipping once.

5. Grill each patty over direct heat for 4 minutes.

6. Flip the patty and brush each top with teriyaki glaze. Grill for another 4 to 5 minutes, or until the internal temperature of the patty reads 155°F with an instant-read thermometer. Add cheese and a pineapple slice to each patty during the last minute of cooking and close the grill lid.

7. Grill the buns over direct-heat, cut side down, for 30 seconds or until marked.

8. Load the buns with the burgers and evenly top with the remaining teriyaki glaze.

BREAKFAST BURGERS

★ **SERVES 4**

★ **INGREDIENTS**

2 pounds ground chuck (80/20)

¾ teaspoon kosher salt

½ teaspoon garlic powder

¼ teaspoon freshly cracked black pepper

8 strips bacon

4 eggs

4 hamburger buns

★ **BEER PAIRING**

Doppelbock

I'm usually a mayo, mustard, and pickle guy when it comes to topping my burgers. However, for this burger I forgo all of those for just one topping: an egg. No extras are needed here. When I top my burgers with an egg and press down slightly on the bun to send the egg yolk cascading down the meat onto the plate, I experience complete bliss. I'll scoop up every last bit of yolk with my burger until everything is gone. I may call it a Breakfast Burger, but it's perfect for any time of day. Feel free to leave those other condiments in the fridge.

1   In a medium bowl, mix together the ground chuck, kosher salt, garlic powder, and black pepper.

2   Divide the mixture into 4 equal-size balls and then press into patties. With your thumb, leave an indentation in the bottom of each patty. This keeps the patty from swelling when on the grill.

3   In a skillet on the stovetop, over medium-low heat, fry 8 strips of bacon until slightly crispy, approximately 8 to 10 minutes, flipping once.

4   In the same skillet, cook the eggs sunny-side up over medium heat until the whites set, approximately 3 to 4 minutes.

5   Prepare a grill for direct medium-high heat, 400° to 500°F.

6   Grill each patty over direct heat for 4 minutes.

7   Flip the patty and grill for another 4 to 5 minutes, or until the internal temperature of the patty reads 155°F with an instant-read thermometer.

8   Grill the buns over direct heat, cut-side down, for 30 seconds or until marked.

9   Fill each bun with a patty, 2 slices of bacon, and an egg.

KOREAN MARINATED
FLAT-IRON STEAK

★ **SERVES 2**

★ **INGREDIENTS**
1 flat-iron steak, 1½ to 2 pounds
½ cup dark lager beer
½ cup extra-virgin olive oil
2 tablespoons gochujang chili paste
2 cloves garlic, chopped
2 cilantro sprigs
½ teaspoon kosher salt
¼ teaspoon freshly cracked black pepper

★ **EQUIPMENT**
One-gallon resealable plastic bag

★ **BEER PAIRING**
Belgian Tripel

When I am looking to add bold and exciting flavors to meat, I make a hard right at the international food aisle of my local grocery store. It's easy to get into routines when grilling, so every once in a while I change things up, and when I do, I go big. Gochujang is a red Korean chili paste. It's part sweet, part savory, and part spicy. There is no mistaking its distinctive flavor. This fermented concoction pairs perfectly with beef, making it a great addition to a marinade. When marinating, using a gallon-size resealable plastic bag is a must. A bowl or dish can work, but forcing the air out of the bag allows more meat and marinade contact. I'm not going to ask you to pronounce it, but I will suggest you put gochujang on your shopping list and give this marinade a try.

1 Place the plastic bag in a bowl and open it. Add all ingredients except the steak to the bag and whisk them together. Add the steak and seal the bag, removing as much air from it as possible. Return the sealed bag to the bowl and refrigerate. Allow the steak to marinate for at least 4 to 6 hours.

2 Remove the steak from the marinade and blot it dry with paper towels. Discard the marinade.

3 Prepare a grill for direct medium-high heat (450° to 500°F).

4 For medium-rare, grill over direct heat for 8 to 10 minutes until the thickest part of the steak reads 125°F with an instant-read thermometer, flipping once.

5 Cut the steak across the grain into thin slices and serve.

REVERSE-SEAR FILET
WITH BLUE CHEESE CRUMBLES

I have a couple of friends who put beef filet at the top of their favorite steak list. In order to achieve a perfect and evenly cooked medium-rare steak, I've taught them to use a reverse sear to achieve this optimal result. A thick beef filet is a perfect cut for this process. Now, in theory, a filet can cook on indirect heat until it's done, but any steak's real flavor is not in the middle of the cut, but in the seared crust. Applying heat by searing the meat produces browning through a chemical process called the Maillard reaction. The browned crust is where all of the flavors are, and it's what keeps you coming back for more. No matter what you grill, do not forget the sear! And the blue cheese? It gives this lean cut just a little something extra to make it perfect.

★ **SERVES 2**

★ **INGREDIENTS**
  2 beef filets, 6 to 8 ounces each
  ½ teaspoon kosher salt
  ½ teaspoon granulated garlic
  ¼ teaspoon freshly cracked black pepper
  Extra-virgin olive oil
  2 ounces blue cheese, crumbled

★ **EQUIPMENT**
  Aluminum foil

★ **BEER PAIRING**
  Imperial IPA

1   Prepare the grill for indirect low heat (200° to 250°F).

2   In a small bowl, combine the salt, garlic, and pepper.

3   Lightly brush the steaks with olive oil. Season all sides with the spice mixture.

4   Grill the filets over indirect heat, until the internal temperature of the filets reads 125°F with an instant-read thermometer, about 20 to 25 minutes.

5   Remove the filets from the grill, tent with aluminum foil, and then allow them to rest.

6   Prepare the grill for direct high heat (450° to 550°F).

7   Grill the filets over high heat for 2 minutes, flipping once. Remove the filets from the grill. Top with the blue cheese. Serve.

GRILLED RIB-EYE
WITH HERB COMPOUND BUTTER

There is nothing I treasure more than a grilled rib-eye. It's the perfect combination of meat and fat, packing in more flavor in one bite than anything else that hits my grill. But as satisfying as rib-eye is on its own, I'm always looking to add just a little more flavor. Have you sensed a theme yet? Instead of adding more seasoning on the prep side, I prepare a compound butter for the finished steak. Compound butter is easy to make and can host a wide range of flavors and additions. This butter is a mix of garlic and fresh herbs and is divine to watch as it melts across the top of a freshly grilled steak. I try to keep a roll of compound butter in the fridge for those days when a rib-eye steak calls to me, which is often!

1   In a small bowl, combine the butter, garlic, rosemary, thyme, salt, and lime zest. Tear off a piece of plastic wrap approximately 8 inches long. Place the butter mixture on one edge of the plastic wrap and roll in the plastic so it resembles a log with the ends sealed. Place in the freezer.

2   Remove any excess fat from the steaks. In a small bowl, combine the salt, paprika, and black pepper. Lightly brush the steaks with olive oil and season all over with the spice rub.

3   Prepare a grill for direct high heat (450° to 550°F).

4   For medium-rare, grill the steaks over high heat until they read 125°F with an instant-read thermometer, approximately 7 to 9 minutes, flipping once.

5   Serve topped with slices of compound butter.

★ **SERVES 2**

★ **INGREDIENTS**
FOR THE COMPOUND BUTTER

½ cup unsalted butter, room temperature

2 cloves garlic, minced

1 teaspoon fresh rosemary, minced

½ teaspoon fresh thyme, minced

¼ teaspoon kosher salt

⅛ teaspoon lime zest

2 rib-eye steaks, 1¼ inches thick

Extra-virgin olive oil

1 teaspoon kosher salt

1 teaspoon smoked paprika

½ teaspoon freshly cracked black pepper

★ **EQUIPMENT**
Plastic wrap

★ **BEER PAIRING**
Oatmeal Stout

PLANKED MEATLOAF

★ **SERVES 4**

★ **INGREDIENTS**

2 pounds ground chuck (80/20)

2 eggs, beaten

1 cup panko bread crumbs

¼ cup chopped shallots

2 cloves garlic, minced

1 tablespoon Worcestershire sauce

1 tablespoon tomato paste

1 teaspoon kosher salt

1 teaspoon ground mustard

1 teaspoon freshly cracked black pepper

¼ cup + 2 tablespoons store-bought BBQ sauce

¼ cup unsalted butter

1 strip bacon, sliced into thirds

★ **EQUIPMENT**

Cedar grilling plank, soaked in water for 30 minutes

★ **BEER PAIRING**

Scotch Ale

When I was a kid, my dad's hectic work schedule forced my mom into the role of head cook. I say forced because cooking was not her passion. However, her four kids needed to eat, and she made it happen. She had her regulars, usually they were chicken dishes, but mom's meatloaf was one of my favorites. It's only been in the last decade that I've brought meatloaf back into my life. It's a great meal and provides terrific leftovers the next day. While my mom's meatloaf cooked away in the oven, I've given mine a home on a smoldering wood plank on a hot grill. When my dad finally retired, my mom retired, too—from cooking. But every once in a while, I ask for meatloaf just for old times' sake, and my inner 12-year-old smiles.

1   In a large bowl, using your hands, combine the meat, eggs, bread crumbs, shallots, garlic, Worcestershire sauce, tomato paste, salt, ground mustard, black pepper, and 2 tablespoons BBQ sauce.

2   Prepare a grill for indirect medium heat (350° to 450°F).

3   In a small saucepan over medium-low heat, combine ¼ cup BBQ sauce and butter until the butter melts. Set the glaze aside.

4   Grill one side of the plank over direct heat until it starts to smolder, about 1 to 2 minutes.

5   Form the meat mixture into a loaf and place it in the center of the burned side of the plank. Top the loaf with the bacon slices.

6   Grill over direct heat until the board begins to smolder, approximately 15 minutes.

7   Move the plank to indirect heat and continue to cook until the internal temperature of the loaf reads 155°F with an instant-read thermometer, approximately 45 to 55 minutes. Brush with glaze every 10 to 15 minutes during cooking.

SMOKED BEEF RIBS

★ **INGREDIENTS**

3 to 5 pounds beef short-plate ribs (usually 4 bones)

FOR THE RUB

2 tablespoons kosher salt

2 tablespoons black pepper

2 tablespoons sugar

Any lager beer to spritz

★ **EQUIPMENT**

Hickory wood chunks or chips

Aluminum foil

Towel

★ **BEER PAIRING**

Barley Wine

The theme of this book is one-beer grilling, so a long meat-smoking session might seem counterintuitive. In this case, the recipe itself is a no-brainer, and the hardest part will be figuring out which glass to use to sip on your Barley Wine. This grill session calls for short-plate ribs, which are my favorite by far. Located on the short-plate primal cut, not far from the skirt and hanger steaks, short-plate ribs are giant and loaded with meat and fat, making for an incredibly tender bite once smoked. There is a reason that in some circles they are called "dinosaur ribs." They are downright huge. Because of their size, they also take a long time to smoke under low heat. But over several hours, the gelatinous fat breaks down, converting these delights from tough to tender. These ribs might be more difficult to source, but a quick chat with your local butcher would be a great first stop.

---

1 With a sharp knife, remove any excess fat from the ribs.

2 In a small bowl, mix together the salt, pepper, and sugar.

3 Season the ribs with the rub, then leave the ribs on the counter while starting the grill.

4 Prepare a grill for indirect low-heat (200° to 250°F). Once at temperature, add a hickory wood chunk to lit briquettes or, on a gas grill, hickory wood chips to a smoker box or foil packet.

5 Smoke the ribs, fat-side up, over indirect heat for 6 to 8 hours, or until the internal temperature of the meat reads 203°F with an instant-read thermometer. During the last 2 hours of cooking, spritz the ribs with beer in a spray bottle to keep the meat moist.

6 Once cooked, cover the ribs with foil, wrap in a towel, and allow to rest 1 hour. Cut between individual bones and serve.

POBLANO BISON SLIDERS

Two things make this recipe stand out: Instead of ground beef, I use ground bison, and instead of a bun, I use smoked poblanos. Transforming a routine recipe like a burger on a bun breathes new life into a staple meal, often making it better than the original. If you've not tried bison, I highly recommend it. It is a leaner, and allegedly healthier, alternative to beef. And these days it's easy to find at most grocery stores. While I love the fat in beef, bison has a unique meaty bite I enjoy. It's different, yet familiar. But the real star here is the poblanos. Charring them and removing the skin brings out the mild, sweet flavor of these large peppers. They are the perfect "bun" for these lip-smacking bison sliders!

1   In a medium bowl, combine the ground bison, salt, and pepper.

2   Prepare a grill for indirect medium heat (350° to 450°F).

3   Grill the peppers over direct heat until the skin is blackened and blistered, approximately 10 minutes, flipping as needed. Seal the peppers in a paper bag and let them sit for 10 to 15 minutes. (Note: Steaming the peppers in the bag makes it easier to remove the charred skin.) Remove the peppers from the bag and peel off the charred skin. Cut the peppers in half and remove the seeds and ribs.

4   Place the pepper halves on a cutting board and top equally with the bison mixture and the goat cheese. Wrap a strip of bacon around each slider.

5   Grill over indirect medium heat until the internal temperature reads 155°F with an instant-read thermometer, approximately 30 to 40 minutes.

★ **SERVES 2**

★ **INGREDIENTS**

1 pound ground bison

½ teaspoon kosher salt

¼ teaspoon freshly cracked black pepper

2 poblano peppers

¼ cup goat cheese

4 strips bacon

★ **EQUIPMENT**

Paper bag

★ **BEER PAIRING**

Irish Red Ale

—— CHAPTER 3 ——

POULTRY

GRILLED CHICKEN SALAD
WITH GREEN GODDESS DRESSING

★ SERVES 4

★ **INGREDIENTS**

FOR THE GREEN GODDESS DRESSING

½ cup mayonnaise

⅓ cup sour cream

2 anchovy fillets

¼ cup Italian parsley

¼ cup cilantro

¼ cup basil

2 tablespoons chives

Zest of 1 lemon

1 tablespoon lemon juice

1 clove garlic

¼ teaspoon sea salt

2 skinless, boneless chicken breasts

1 teaspoon extra-virgin olive oil

½ teaspoon kosher salt

¼ teaspoon freshly cracked black pepper

2 romaine lettuce heads, chopped

1 avocado, pitted and diced

½ cup grape tomatoes, quartered

1 cup canned black beans, drained and rinsed

★ **BEER PAIRING**

Helles

If I am going to make a salad, you can guarantee I will work the grill into it. Thanks to grilled chicken, it will not be a side, it will be a meal. While I'm not ordinarily a big fan of skinless, boneless chicken breasts as the focus of a dish, they are a great add-on when they have that perfect char from the grill. The grilled chicken is partly why I love this salad so much. The other is the herby green goddess dressing. It's plenty easy to pick up a bottle of this dressing at the grocery store. But when you make your own, the difference in taste is astounding. The brightness of the fresh herbs matched with the tender cuts of grilled chicken make this a salad worth repeating.

1   In a food processor or blender, pulse the dressing ingredients until the herbs are minced. Transfer the contents to a small bowl.

2   Remove any excess fat from the chicken breasts. Brush with olive oil and season with salt and pepper.

3   Prepare a grill for direct medium heat (350° to 450°F).

4   Grill the chicken breasts over direct heat until the internal temperature reads 165°F with an instant-read thermometer, approximately 8 to 12 minutes, flipping once.

5   Remove chicken from the grill and slice into strips.

6   Arrange the chopped lettuce on a large platter. Top with the chicken, avocado, tomatoes, and black beans. Serve with the dressing.

SPATCHCOCKED CHICKEN

When I first heard the term "spatchcock," I wasn't entirely sure what I was getting myself into. While the origin of the term is murky—it may be of Irish origin—the benefit of spatchcocking is profound. Spatchcocking is the process of removing a chicken's (or turkey's) backbone to allow the bird to lie flat on the grill. With increased surface area that is exposed to heat, a spatchcocked chicken will grill faster and, in my opinion, taste better than a traditionally grilled bird. It might sound like major surgery, but the backbone removal process is easily accomplished with a sturdy pair of kitchen scissors or a sharp knife. This is my go-to method for grilling a whole chicken, and after you give it a shot I have a feeling it will be yours too.

1   Place the chicken breast-side down. With a pair of kitchen scissors or a sharp knife, cut down each side of the backbone and remove it. Flip the chicken over, placing the exposed cavity down. Press down on the chicken until the breastbone breaks and the chicken lies flat.

2   In a small bowl, combine the salt, thyme, onion powder, black pepper, and lemon zest.

3   Brush the chicken with olive oil and season with the rub.

4   Prepare a grill for indirect medium-high heat (400° to 450°F).

5   Grill the chicken over indirect medium-high heat, skin side up, until the internal temperature of the breast reads 165°F with an instant-read thermometer.

★ **SERVES 4**

★ **INGREDIENTS**
1 whole chicken, 4 to 5 pounds

FOR THE RUB
1 teaspoon kosher salt
1 teaspoon dried thyme
½ teaspoon onion powder
½ teaspoon freshly cracked black pepper
Zest of one lemon

1 tablespoon extra-virgin olive oil

★ **EQUIPMENT**
Kitchen scissors

★ **BEER PAIRING**
Witbier

SUNDAY WHOLE CHICKEN

Sundays are my days to grill a whole chicken. Grilling them whole is more economical than buying just pieces, and the flavor from Sunday Whole Chicken is far superior. Plus, the remaining carcass is perfect for making stock for soups or sauces. It's a meal on a meal on a meal! See the Chicken Quesadillas on page 60 or the Grilled Chicken Salad on page 68. Aside from the benefit of providing lots of succulent meat, grilling a whole chicken is straight-up simple. It's just a trussed chicken on a grate smoking away to perfection while you sit back and enjoy a cold one. That smoke goes a long way, too: just a small amount of smoldering wood turns the skin a perfect caramel color for a great-looking and tasting bird.

---

1 In a small bowl, combine the salt, thyme, tarragon, and black pepper.

2 Brush the chicken with olive oil and season all over with the rub.

3 Remove the wingtips. Truss the chicken with butcher twine by tying together the legs and then running the twine to the neck to secure the wings.

4 Prepare a grill for indirect medium heat (350° to 450°F)

5 Once at temperature, add a hickory wood chunk to lit briquettes or, on a gas grill, hickory wood chips to a smoker box or foil packet.

6 Grill the chicken until the internal temperature of the breast reads 165°F with an instant-read thermometer, approximately 1 hour to 1 hour and 15 minutes.

★ **SERVES 4**

★ **INGREDIENTS**
1 whole chicken, 4 to 5 pounds

FOR THE RUB
1 teaspoon kosher salt
1 teaspoon dried thyme
½ teaspoon dried tarragon
½ teaspoon freshly cracked black pepper

1 tablespoon extra-virgin olive oil

★ **EQUIPMENT**
Butcher twine
Hickory wood chunks or chips

★ **BEER PAIRING**
Dunkelweizen

CHICKEN QUESADILLAS

★ **SERVES 2**

★ **INGREDIENTS**

2 flour tortillas

1 cup chopped grilled chicken

2 cups shredded cheddar

⅔ cups queso fresco, crumbled

¼ cup red onion, diced

8 grape tomatoes, quartered

2 tablespoons cilantro, chopped

Hot sauce

1 tablespoon extra-virgin olive oil

★ **BEER PAIRING**

Oatmeal Stout

Open my refrigerator on any random day and there is one thing you will always see (apart from beer, of course): tortillas. Flour tortillas are the perfect vessel for so many foods. Sometimes, I use them for meals from scratch, like these quesadillas. Other times, they make leftovers shine by allowing me to enjoy last night's meal in a different way. Grilled quesadillas are easy to prepare and open to a wide variety of ingredients. Here I've kept it simple, using some of my favorite ingredients, the most important being the cheeses. I often use both soft and hard cheeses for flavor and texture. The cheddar makes for the perfect creamy melt while the queso fresco gives a firm, salty bite. Before grilling, be sure to brush the tortillas with olive oil to keep them from sticking. Proper grill temperature is a must. It should be hot enough to melt the cheese, but not so hot it burns the tortillas. These cook fast, so grab a beer and stay grill side while you crank them out.

1   Load half of each tortilla with chicken, cheddar, queso fresco, onion, tomatoes, cilantro, and a few dashes of hot sauce. Fold the tortilla in half and brush both sides with olive oil.

2   Prepare a grill for direct medium heat (350° to 450°F).

3   Grill the quesadillas over direct heat until marked and the cheese has melted, approximately 2 to 3 minutes, flipping once.

4   Remove, cut into pieces, and serve.

CHICKEN-BACON-RANCH
SANDWICHES

I eat a lot of beef; so much that it's easy to forget how good a perfectly cooked chicken breast can be. The key to the last statement is "perfectly cooked," meaning cooked to the right temperature. For chicken, it means 165°F as measured by an instant-read thermometer. Hitting the perfect temperature is like Goldilocks finding porridge; it has to be just right. Chicken breasts are not always uniform in thickness, which makes it a challenge to cook them evenly. To remedy this, use a heavy-bottomed kitchen pan or a meat mallet to pound the breasts to an even thickness. A little extra work ahead of the cooking can only yield success, and a tender, juicy grilled chicken breast makes Chicken-Bacon-Ranch Sandwiches shine.

★ **SERVES 2**

★ **INGREDIENTS**

2 skinless, boneless chicken breasts

1 teaspoon extra-virgin olive oil

½ teaspoon kosher salt

½ teaspoon granulated garlic

¼ teaspoon freshly cracked black pepper

4 strips bacon

2 potato burger buns

Store-bought ranch dressing

½ cup mixed greens

★ **BEER PAIRING**
American Lager

1   Remove any excess fat from the chicken breasts and brush them with the olive oil. In a small bowl, combine the salt, garlic, and black pepper, then evenly season the chicken.

2   In a skillet on the stove top over medium-low heat, cook 4 strips of bacon until slightly crispy, approximately 8 to 10 minutes, flipping once.

3   Prepare a grill for direct medium heat (350° to 450°F).

4   Grill the chicken breasts over direct heat until the internal temperature reads 165°F with an instant-read thermometer, approximately 8 to 12 minutes, flipping once.

5   Grill the buns cut-side down over direct heat until marked, approximately 1 minute.

6   Load the buns with the chicken, bacon, ranch dressing, and mixed greens.

STUFFED CHICKEN BREASTS
WITH HERBS AND GOAT CHEESE

★ **SERVES 4**

★ **INGREDIENTS**

4 skinless, boneless chicken breasts

3 ounces goat cheese

2 tablespoons unsalted butter, room temperature

1½ teaspoons chives, minced

1 teaspoon Italian parsley, minced

¼ teaspoon fresh thyme, minced

¼ teaspoon lemon juice

1 clove garlic, minced

1 tablespoon extra-virgin olive oil

1 teaspoon kosher salt

½ teaspoon freshly cracked black pepper

★ **BEER PAIRING**
Imperial Red Ale

It's no secret that the best-tasting meat on the chicken is the dark meat found in the thighs. I still remember my dad serving grilled chicken and asking, "White meat or dark meat?" The kids went for the white breasts and the adults went for the dark thighs and legs. Now I know why! Thankfully, lean breasts are perfect for taking on countless fresh ingredients that ramp up their flavor. I like to go big with goat cheese and garlic, but feel free to change up the stuffing to your favorites. It takes a little more time, but stuffing chicken breasts is a great way to take the leanest part of the chicken to the next level.

1 Create a pocket in each chicken breast by cutting through the long side of the breast, in the middle of the flesh, with a sharp knife. Work the knife in short strokes, being careful not to cut all of the way through.

2 In a small bowl, combine the cheese, butter, chives, parsley, thyme, lemon juice, and garlic.

3 Stuff each breast with the cheese mixture.

4 Brush the chicken breasts with olive oil and season with salt and pepper.

5 Prepare a grill for direct medium heat (350° to 450°F).

6 Grill the chicken breasts over direct heat until the internal temperature reads 165°F with an instant-read thermometer, flipping once, approximately 8 to 10 minutes.

STUFFED CHICKEN BREASTS
WITH PROSCIUTTO AND FONTINA

When I was growing up, my mom made so many different chicken dishes I had to number them, as it was easier to remember the number than the name. It's not surprising; chicken is incredibly versatile, inexpensive, and, when paired with bold flavors and textures, delicious. This recipe is almost a sandwich in a chicken breast, with layers of prosciutto, cheese, and red pepper guaranteed in every slice of chicken. I recommend using toothpicks to keep the cavity shut during grilling because the fontina cheese melts readily, but butcher twine is an easy substitute. Just be sure to remove them before serving.

1 Create a pocket in each chicken breast by taking a sharp knife and slicing evenly through the long side of the breast, in the center of the flesh. Work the knife in short strokes, being careful not to cut all of the way through.

2 Stuff each breast with prosciutto, red pepper, 2 basil leaves, and cheese.

3 Using toothpicks, "sew" the opening shut by weaving the toothpicks through the flesh to close the pocket.

4 Prepare a grill for direct medium heat (350° to 450°F).

5 Grill the chicken breasts over direct heat until the internal temperature reads 165°F with an instant-read thermometer, flipping once, approximately 8 to 10 minutes.

6 Remove from the grill. Remove the toothpicks and serve.

★ **SERVES 3**

★ **INGREDIENTS**
3 skinless, boneless chicken breasts

3 slices prosciutto

3 roasted red pepper slices, about 1 by 3 inches

6 basil leaves

8 ounces fontina cheese, grated

¾ teaspoon kosher salt

½ teaspoon freshly cracked black pepper

★ **EQUIPMENT**
9 wooden toothpicks

★ **BEER PAIRING**
Brown Ale

SMOKED CHICKEN WINGS

SERVES: 4

★ **INGREDIENTS**

12 chicken wings, about 3 pounds

1 tablespoon extra-virgin olive oil

½ teaspoon kosher salt

¼ teaspoon freshly ground black pepper

½ cup hot sauce of your choice

½ cup unsalted butter

★ **EQUIPMENT**

Cherry wood chunks or chips

★ **BEER PAIRING**

Sour

I don't know for sure, but I am willing to bet we share a love for smoked chicken wings. Just the thought of tender meat wrapped in a crispy, hot-sauce-bathed skin sends a Pavlovian signal that turns me toward the grill. I prepare wings in a two-part process, starting with a low-temperature smoke, slowly bringing them close to cooked temperature. After a quick toss in sauce, the wings return to the grill for a high-temperature sear. The end results are wings that are both tender and crispy. I've paired Smoked Chicken Wings with a classic hot sauce, but the grilling process is open to whatever choice of sauce your taste buds desire. I can easily make these again and again. I'm sure you will, too.

1 Separate the wings, drumettes, and wingtips. Discard the wingtips. In a large bowl, toss the chicken with the olive oil, salt, and black pepper.

2 In a small saucepan, heat the hot sauce and butter over medium heat until the butter has melted. Reduce heat to low and keep warm.

3 Prepare a grill for indirect low heat (200° to 250°F).

4 Once at temperature, add a cherry wood chunk to lit briquettes or, on a gas grill, cherry wood chips to a smoker box or foil packet.

5 Grill the wings over indirect heat until the internal temperature of the wings reads 160°F with an instant-read thermometer, approximately 20 to 25 minutes.

6 Remove from the grill and toss with half the sauce.

7 Prepare a grill for direct medium-high heat (450° to 500°F).

8 Grill the wings over direct medium-high heat until marked, approximately 1 minute, flipping once.

9 Toss with the remaining sauce and serve.

GRILLED CHICKEN SALAD

★ **SERVES 4**

★ **INGREDIENTS**

1 Sunday Whole Chicken (page 59), chopped (makes about 4 cups)

1 cup mayonnaise

2 teaspoons Dijon mustard

1 cup quartered grapes

2 celery stalks, diced

½ cup chopped walnuts

2 tablespoons fresh lemon juice

½ cup dried cranberries

1 teaspoon Tabasco sauce

½ teaspoon kosher salt

¼ teaspoon freshly cracked black pepper

★ **BEER PAIRING**

Cream Ale

If my Sunday Whole Chicken is the gift that keeps on giving, call this Grilled Chicken Salad one of its best gifts. I make this salad a few times a month, and it's often the destination for the entire chicken. Grilled Chicken Salad is great for busy weeks when I want an easy make-ahead lunch or a welcomed last-minute dinner. Packed with flavor and texture, not just from the chicken, but also from the walnuts, grapes, and cranberries, it has a lot going for it. While the recipe calls for chopping the chicken, it's easy to shred it by pulling the still-warm chicken meat off the bone and into a stand mixer. Run the mixer on slow with a paddle attachment, so that the chicken effortlessly shreds, making it easier to mix in with the ingredients and providing a more uniform bite.

1   In a large bowl, combine all of the ingredients with a wooden spoon.

2   Cover and refrigerate for at least 4 hours to allow the flavors to meld.

GRILLED CHICKEN WRAPS
WITH CHIPOTLE MAYONNAISE

Sure, you could use leftover grilled chicken for this recipe, but I like to grill fresh chicken breasts. Tender, warm, freshly grilled pieces of chicken make a huge difference. The flour tortilla is once again clinching the award for the best ingredient in a supporting role, but the real star here is the chipotle mayonnaise. At all times, I keep a can of chipotle peppers in adobo sauce tucked away in the pantry. Chipotles are dried and smoked jalapeños, and when immersed in tangy adobo sauce they are the pinnacle of culinary beauty. The chipotle mayonnaise in this recipe brings these flavors to the forefront, adding some heat to the wraps without being overpowering.

1 Remove any excess fat from the chicken breasts. Brush with olive oil and season with salt and pepper.

2 In a small bowl, combine the mayonnaise and pureed chipotle peppers. Set aside.

3 Prepare a grill for direct medium heat (350° to 450°F).

4 Grill the chicken breasts over direct heat until the internal temperature reads 165°F with an instant-read thermometer, approximately 8 to 12 minutes, flipping once.

5 Remove from the grill and roughly chop.

6 Spread the mayonnaise mixture on one-half of each tortilla. Load the same half of each tortilla with equal parts chicken, cheese, banana peppers, and lettuce.

7 Tightly roll each tortilla like a burrito, then cut in half and serve.

★ **SERVES 4**

★ **INGREDIENTS**

2 skinless, boneless chicken breasts

1 teaspoon extra-virgin olive oil

½ teaspoon kosher salt

¼ teaspoon freshly cracked black pepper

½ cup mayonnaise

2 teaspoons pureed chipotle peppers with adobo sauce

4 flour tortillas

1 cup shredded Asiago cheese

½ cup store-bought, sliced banana peppers

6 romaine lettuce leaves, chopped

★ **BEER PAIRING**

Belgian Dubel

CHICKEN CHEESESTEAK
SANDWICHES

I love a good cheesesteak. It's literally a balanced meal in every bite: protein, vegetables, dairy, and grains. However, what happens when you swap out the steak in cheesesteak for chicken? Is it a cheese-chicken, a grilled chicken cheese, or what I call a grilled chicken cheesesteak? No matter the title, this grilled medley of vegetables layered with tender slices of chicken, topped with a gooey layer of provolone cheese and nestled in a grilled hoagie bun, really ticks all the boxes. The only thing left to grab is a golden strong ale to wash it down. Its subtle citrus notes and cloudy appearance are the perfect match for this rich sandwich.

1   Prepare a griddle on the grill for direct medium-high heat, 400° to 500°F.

2   Warm half of the oil on the griddle and add the peppers and onions. Lower the lid. Stir occasionally and cook until the vegetables are soft, about 7 to 8 minutes.

3   Toss the chicken slices with BBQ rub and salt. Push the vegetables to the back of the griddle. Add the remaining oil to the front and warm. Add the chicken slices. Lower the lid. Stirring occasionally, cook the chicken until it's cooked through, about 6 to 8 minutes.

4   Spread the mayonnaise on the open buns and grill over direct medium heat until browned, about 1 minute.

5   Mix the chicken and vegetables together to form a single, even layer. Top the mixture with overlapping slices of provolone cheese. Lower the lid and allow the cheese to melt, about 1 to 2 minutes.

6   With a spatula, remove the cheesesteaks from the grill and load the hoagie buns. Serve.

★ **SERVES 3**

★ **INGREDIENTS**
2 tablespoons vegetable oil, divided
1 onion, sliced
1 green pepper, sliced
2 red peppers, sliced
3 skinless, boneless chicken breasts, sliced
3 tablespoons BBQ rub
½ teaspoon kosher salt
6 slices provolone cheese
3 hoagie buns
2 tablespoons mayonnaise

★ **EQUIPMENT**
Griddle

★ **BEER PAIRING**
Golden Strong Ale

BEER-CAN CHICKEN

★ **INGREDIENTS**

1 whole chicken, 4 to 5 pounds

FOR THE RUB

1 teaspoon kosher salt

1 teaspoon granulated garlic

½ teaspoon freshly cracked black pepper

½ teaspoon ground cumin

½ teaspoon ground coriander

¼ teaspoon red pepper flakes

1 12-ounce canned lager beer

1 tablespoon extra-virgin olive oil

★ **BEER PAIRING**

English-Style IPA

When I entertain, my go-to grilled chicken is Beer-Can Chicken. There is endless Internet debate on whether this is the "best" way to cook a chicken. Does the can really make a difference? Is it more tender? Juicier? My answer is, I don't know, and I don't care; I just think it looks awesome. For me, Beer-Can Chicken is about the presentation. I know the chicken will be good, but there is something very cool, and funny, about seeing a chicken sit atop a beer-can throne, smoking away. Guests love it when the grill lid pulls away to reveal the wings-back chicken ready for the dinner table. Is it the best-grilled chicken method ever? Who's to say? I just know that in the moment it's perfect for me, and I hope for you, too.

1 In a small bowl, combine the dry ingredients to make the rub.

2 Prepare a grill for indirect medium heat (350° to 450°F).

3 Open the beer and take a few sips. With a can opener, make two additional openings in the top of the beer can.

4 Brush the chicken with olive oil and season all over with the rub.

5 Place the beer can on a tray or sheet pan and then place the chicken, cavity-side-down, over the can. Bring the legs forward for balance and tuck the wings behind the chicken's back.

6 Grill the chicken over indirect medium heat until the internal temperature of the breast reads 165°F with an instant-read thermometer, approximately 1 hour to 1 hour and 15 minutes. Note: Depending on the size of the grill, consider tenting parts of the chicken with aluminum foil if the skin starts to char.

ASIAN GLAZED
CHICKEN THIGHS

Whenever I grill chicken thighs, I always ask myself why I don't grill them more often. Unlike white breast meat, the dark thigh meat is resilient on the grill and hard to overcook. Plus, I always opt for chicken thighs with skin and bone. Boneless thighs might be easier to grill, but the added flavor from the bone and the crispy skin makes it well worth the trouble. Thighs are great with just a light seasoning, but there is always more flavor to add, so I've added an Asian inspired glaze. This recipe showcases the importance of a two-zone fire, both direct and indirect heat. Here, the direct heat is perfect for crisping the skin and providing the initial sear. However, indirect heat is a must to finish the cook, especially with the glaze. Sugar easily burns over direct heat, so the thighs would experience flare-ups and excessive burning without the indirect zone. Master the zones, and you master the grill.

★ **SERVES 4**

★ **INGREDIENTS**
FOR THE GLAZE
½ cup soy sauce

½ cup dark brown sugar

1 tablespoon rice vinegar

1 clove garlic, minced

1 teaspoon cornstarch

4 skin-on, bone-in chicken thighs

1 teaspoon extra-virgin olive oil

¾ teaspoon kosher salt

¼ teaspoon freshly cracked black pepper

★ **BEER PAIRING**
English ESB

1   In a small saucepan on the stovetop, bring the glaze ingredients to a boil over high heat. Reduce the heat and simmer until the sauce thickens, approximately 8 to 10 minutes. Set aside.

2   Remove any excess fat or skin from the chicken thighs. Brush with the olive oil and season with salt and pepper.

3   Prepare a grill for indirect medium heat (350° to 450°F).

4   Grill the thighs over direct medium heat, skin-side down, until the skin is marked, approximately 6 minutes. Flip the thighs and grill over indirect heat until the internal temperature of the meat reads 165°F with an instant-read thermometer, approximately 25 to 30 minutes, basting with the glaze every 10 minutes.

BUTTERMILK-MARINATED
CHICKEN SKEWERS

★ **SERVES 4**

★ **INGREDIENTS**

2 cups buttermilk

2 cloves garlic, minced

2 tablespoons Italian parsley, chopped

1 teaspoon smoked paprika

3 boneless, skinless chicken breasts, cut into 1-inch cubes

1 red bell pepper

1 green bell pepper

½ sweet onion

★ **EQUIPMENT**

One-gallon resealable plastic bag

Metal skewers, or wooden skewers soaked in water 30 minutes or more

★ **BEER PAIRING**

German Schwarzbier

Buttermilk is an excellent marinade for chicken. Its acidic makeup helps tenderize the meat and break down proteins, creating tender bite after tender bite. Cutting the chicken into small cubes means more surface area for the buttermilk marinade to ramp up the flavor of every bite. Skewers are the ideal accessories to control smaller pieces of meat on the grill, and because we are using skewers, adding vegetables is a no-brainer. Metal skewers are ideal, but thick wooden skewers soaked in water at least 30 minutes before grilling work just as well. Be sure to leave space around the skewered meat to promote even cooking. Skewering meat and vegetables can take time, so I always encourage my guests help build their own. Besides, when you take ownership of a skewer, it tends to taste even better, or so my guests tell me!

1 Place the plastic bag in a bowl. Add the buttermilk to the bag and whisk in the garlic, parsley, and paprika. Add the chicken to the bag. Remove the air and seal. Refrigerate 6 to 8 hours.

2 Cut the peppers into planks, then into 1-inch square pieces. Cut the onion half in half again and separate layers into 1-inch pieces.

3 Load the skewers with alternate layers of chicken, onion, and peppers.

4 Prepare a grill for direct medium heat (350° to 450°F).

5 Grill the skewers over direct heat until the internal temperature of the chicken reads 165°F with an instant-read thermometer, approximately 8 to 10 minutes, rotating the skewers several times.

CHAPTER 4
PORK

SMOKED PORK CHILI

One of my mantras is to "take it outside." If you can make it in the kitchen, you can make it on the grill. The grill only makes it better. Chili is a perfect example. I've certainly made my fair share of chili on the stovetop, but the same recipe, like Smoked Pork Chili, takes on a completely different character when it's moved to the grill. The chili absorbs the wafting smoke, adding even more flavor to this bountiful recipe. I use a cast-iron Dutch oven when I'm making chili or soup on the grill. Whatever you use, be sure it's fireproof. Also, leave the lid off the pot but keep the grill lid down as much as possible. Stirring every 15 minutes or so helps work the trapped smoke back into the chili.

---

1 In the Dutch oven over medium heat on the stovetop, heat the olive oil and then sweat the vegetables until soft, approximately 3 to 4 minutes.

2 Add the ground pork and cook until browned, approximately 10 to 12 minutes.

3 Stir in the seasonings, tomatoes, and beer, and bring to a boil over high heat.

4 Prepare a grill for indirect low heat (200° to 250°F).

5 Once at temperature, add 2 or 3 hickory wood chunks to lit briquettes or, on a gas grill, hickory wood chips to a smoker box or foil packet.

6 Once the grill begins to smoke, cook the chili over indirect heat for an hour, stirring occasionally.

7 Remove and serve with cheese and jalapeño slices.

★ **SERVES 8**

★ **INGREDIENTS**
1 tablespoon extra-virgin olive oil

1 red bell pepper, diced

1 green bell pepper, diced

1 sweet onion, medium, diced

2 pounds ground pork

3 tablespoons chili powder

2 tablespoons dark brown sugar

1 tablespoon cumin

1 tablespoon paprika

1 teaspoon oregano

1 teaspoon mustard powder

½ teaspoon cinnamon

½ teaspoon kosher salt

¼ teaspoon freshly cracked black pepper

2 cans diced tomatoes

1 12-ounce strong ale beer

1 cup grated pepper jack cheese

1 jalapeño, sliced

★ **EQUIPMENT**
Cast-iron Dutch oven

Hickory wood chunk or chips

★ **BEER PAIRING**
Rauchbier

BBQ BREAKFAST "FATTY"

★ SERVES 4

★ INGREDIENTS
1 pound pork sausage

1 pound bacon

3 hardboiled eggs

2 tablespoons store-bought BBQ rub, divided

½ cup grated cheddar cheese

½ cup grated Swiss cheese

★ EQUIPMENT
One-gallon resealable plastic bag

Rolling pin

Plastic wrap

Applewood chunks or chips

★ BEER PAIRING
Breakfast Stout

I recently hosted friends to record an episode of their food podcast, *The Meat Bucket*. Along with the many grilled delicacies I was preparing, I mentioned smoking a fatty. I detected a noticeable pause in the conversation. Amused, I explained that a BBQ fatty is an old pitmaster staple. It's a pound of ground pork sausage, stuffed and wrapped in a weave of delicious bacon. Smoking one of these will not send you to jail, but might send you for blood work at the doctor's! A fatty can be stuffed with just about anything, and here I include three hardboiled eggs, making it a complete breakfast. Coming off the grill, this pork feast always wows guests. Just make sure everyone is expecting the same fatty.

1 Place the pork sausage in the plastic bag and roll it flat with a rolling pin.

2 With a knife, cut down both sides of the bag, creating a flap. Open the flap to expose the sausage.

3 Make a bacon weave by alternating eight strips by eight strips of bacon on a large sheet of plastic wrap.

4 Season the bacon weave with 1 tablespoon of the BBQ rub.

5 Remove the pork from the bag and place over half of the bacon weave.

6 Line up the hardboiled eggs close to the pork sausage and bacon edge.

7 Using the plastic wrap as an assist, roll the weave up, starting with the pork sausage and egg side. Continue to roll until you have a cylindrical "loaf."

8 Roll the wrap to seal the sides and place it in the refrigerator.

9 Prepare a grill for indirect low heat (200° to 250°F).

10 Once at temperature, add 2 or 3 applewood chunks to the lit briquettes or, on a gas grill, applewood chips to a smoker box or foil packet.

11 Remove the fatty from the plastic wrap and season with the BBQ rub.

12 Once the grill starts to smoke, grill the fatty over indirect low heat until the internal temperature of the pork reads 160°F with an instant-read thermometer, approximately 50 to 60 minutes.

SMOKED PULLED PORK

★ SERVES 8

★ INGREDIENTS
1 pork butt, 6 to 8 pounds

FOR THE RUB
2 tablespoons dark brown sugar

2 tablespoons sweet paprika

1 teaspoon cumin

1 teaspoon garlic

1 teaspoon freshly cracked
black pepper

1 teaspoon kosher salt

½ teaspoon ground mustard

⅛ teaspoon celery seed

½ teaspoon ancho chili powder

★ EQUIPMENT
Applewood chunks or chips

★ BEER PAIRING
Marzen

While many of these recipes are quick to prepare and grill, this one takes some time, but don't let it scare you away. Look at it as a way to have more than one beer. The time and effort pay off, not only for this meal, but also for wonderful leftovers for days after. Pulled pork was the first authentic BBQ I learned to master, and rightfully so. A pork butt is a relatively cheap cut of meat and can feed a huge group of people. I love it for entertaining and always hope there will be leftovers. But I'm never really surprised when there are none. While I've smoked pork butts on gas grills, this is really a recipe for a charcoal grill or smoker. Live fire truly enhances the process. The charcoal-fueled smoke paints the pork a beautiful, luscious mahogany, and when cooked, the shoulder blade smoothly slides out.

1   In a small bowl, combine the rub ingredients. Cover the pork butt in rub.

2   Prepare the grill for indirect low heat (200° to 250°F). Note: This recipe works best on a charcoal grill or smoker. But that being said, it is entirely possible to make great BBQ on a gas grill. Also, this is a long cook, so make sure you have plenty of fuel on hand. If grilling with charcoal, stack approximately 90 unlit coals under 20 lit coals. The coals will slowly burn down the stack of unlit coals, maintaining a low temperature for hours.

3   Once at temperature, add 2 or 3 applewood chunks to lit briquettes or, on a gas grill, applewood chips to a smoker box or foil packet.

4   Once the grill begins to smoke, grill the pork butt over indirect heat for 7 to 9 hours, or until the internal temperature of the pork reads 203°F with an instant-read thermometer. The pork shoulder blade should pull cleanly from the meat and the meat should easily pull apart with your hands or a pair of forks.

BBQ PORK
STUFFED PEPPERS

When I'm lucky enough to have leftover pulled pork, I'm always looking for different ways to use it. Often, it ends up in quesadillas or tacos, but one of my favorite ways is stuffed into bell peppers. This is a solid, after-work, last-minute meal using ingredients already on hand. It's a meal I go to when I want an excuse to fire up the grill and drink a beer or two, because it takes just a little bit of prep and a little bit of time. The easiest way to stuff the peppers is to split them in half vertically. As a variation, it is possible to slice the pepper top off and stuff them standing up. In that case, be sure to select peppers with flat bottoms to avoid their falling over on the grill.

★ **SERVES 3**

★ **INGREDIENTS**

3 bell peppers

1 pound pulled pork
(cooked, but not reheated)

½ cup store-bought BBQ sauce

3 strips bacon, sliced lengthwise
and cut in half

6 slices smoked Gouda cheese

★ **BEER PAIRING**

Belgian Quadrupel

1   Slice the peppers in half vertically from the stem to the bottom. Scoop out the seeds and ribs. Note: When buying peppers, try to select ones relatively uniform in shape and size.

2   In a medium bowl, combine the pork and BBQ sauce. Fill the pepper halves with equal amounts of pork.

3   Top the pork with a slice of cheese and two pieces of the sliced bacon.

4   Preheat the grill for indirect medium heat (350° to 450°F).

5   Grill the peppers over indirect medium heat until the bacon has rendered, the peppers are cooked, and the pork is heated through, approximately 30 to 40 minutes.

SWEET MUSTARD-GLAZED
PORK TENDERLOIN

Pork tenderloin is a very lean cut of meat with one requirement for success: a correct final cook temperature. All of the flavor and seasoning in the world will not help an overcooked pork tenderloin. In the old days, pork was usually overcooked, thanks to the lingering fear of catching trichinosis from undercooked pork. Thanks to improved laws governing food production, trichinosis has been virtually eliminated, meaning it's safe to eat pork at a much better-tasting internal temperature of 145°F. A perfectly cooked pork tenderloin is delicious and aptly suited to take on additional flavor in the form of glazes or rubs. Sweet Mustard-Glazed Pork Tenderloin showcases one of my favorite glazes, which offers just a touch of seasoned heat. Usually, a tenderloin works great over direct heat, but here the sweet glaze works best over indirect to avoid flare-ups.

★ **SERVES 4**

★ **INGREDIENTS**

2 tablespoons dark brown sugar

2 tablespoons Dijon mustard

1 pork tenderloin

1 teaspoon kosher salt

½ teaspoon freshly cracked black pepper

¼ teaspoon ancho chili powder

★ **EQUIPMENT**

Aluminum foil

★ **BEER PAIRING**

Maibock

1   In a small bowl, combine the brown sugar and mustard.

2   Remove any excess fat and silver skin from the tenderloin.

3   Season the tenderloin with salt, black pepper, and chili powder. Brush all over with the glaze.

4   Prepare a grill for indirect medium heat (350° to 450°F).

5   Grill the tenderloin over indirect heat until the internal temperature reads 145°F with an instant-read thermometer, approximately 25 to 35 minutes.

6   Remove from the grill, tent with aluminum foil, and allow to rest for 5 minutes. Slice into 1-inch pieces and serve.

SMOKED BABY BACK RIBS
WITH TANGY BBQ SAUCE

★ **SERVES 8**

★ **INGREDIENTS**
3 racks back ribs

FOR THE RUB
2 tablespoons dark brown sugar
2 tablespoons sweet paprika
1 teaspoon cumin
1 teaspoon garlic
1 teaspoon freshly cracked black pepper
1 teaspoon kosher salt
½ teaspoon ground mustard
⅛ teaspoon celery seed
½ teaspoon ancho chili powder

FOR THE SAUCE
1 cup ketchup
2 tablespoons pineapple juice
1 tablespoon dark molasses
1 tablespoon honey
1 teaspoon sweet paprika
1 teaspoon Worcestershire sauce
½ teaspoon chipotle chili powder

★ **EQUIPMENT**
Applewood chunks or chips
Rib rack
Basting brush

★ **BEER PAIRING**
Milk Stout

Unless I go to a true BBQ joint, I never order ribs at a restaurant. Ever. Once you smoke ribs at home, you will see why. Something special happens when rubbed pork meets smoldering wood over the low heat of the grill. It is an investment in time for sure, but it is my kind of BBQ, giving me a chance to open a beer and just be with the grill as the magic happens. As times goes on, the pork fat slowly renders, transforming the meat between the ribs into tender bites. "Fall off the bone" meat is not authentic smoked BBQ. Real BBQ is tender but has a slight amount of resistance as the meat tears away. There is no mistaking it, and once you smoke ribs in your backyard, you'll understand why nothing is better.

1   Remove the papery membrane from the back side of the ribs: With the ribs meat-side down, slide a dull knife between the membrane and a bone in the middle of the rack to create room for a finger. Insert a finger all the way under the membrane and then, by pulling up, remove the membrane from the entire rack.

2   In a small bowl, combine the rub ingredients. Season the ribs all over with the rub.

3   Prepare a grill for indirect low heat (200° to 250°F).

4   Once at temperature, add 2 or 3 applewood chunks to lit briquettes or, on a gas grill, applewood chips to a smoker box or foil packet.

5   Depending on the size of your grill, consider the use of a rib rack to keep the ribs vertical and to maintain space while cooking.

6   In a small saucepan on the stovetop, bring the sauce ingredients to a boil over medium-high heat. Reduce heat to low and simmer for 30 minutes. Remove from the stove and allow to cool.

7   Grill the ribs over low heat until the meat around the bones begins to retract at least a half-inch and the rack can easily be bent back over itself, approximately 4 to 5 hours. Baste with sauce the last hour of cooking.

MAPLE-GLAZED
PORK TENDERLOINS

I've already touched on the importance of grilling pork tenderloins to the correct internal temperature. It will seriously make the difference between an unforgettable meal and one you might want to forget. Another tip for great grilled tenderloin is to trim the meat. Pork tenderloin is not ready for the grill the minute it leaves the package. Before grilling, always remove any excess fat and the silver skin. The silver skin is the striated membrane running along the sides of the meat. It is connective tissue and not edible, so it needs to come off. Run a sharp knife directly under the skin and cut horizontally to remove it. Make thin cuts, being careful not to remove too much pork meat. The pork is now ready for the grill, and slathering on the sweet maple glaze takes this tenderloin from good to great.

★ **SERVES 4**

★ **INGREDIENTS**
1 pork tenderloin
1 teaspoon extra-virgin olive oil
1 teaspoon kosher salt
½ teaspoon freshly cracked black pepper
3 tablespoons maple syrup
2 tablespoons apple cider vinegar
1 teaspoon Dijon mustard

★ **EQUIPMENT**
Aluminum foil

★ **BEER PAIRING**
New England IPA

1 Remove any excess fat and silver skin from the tenderloin.

2 Brush the tenderloin with olive oil and season with salt and pepper.

3 In a small bowl, combine the maple syrup, cider vinegar, and Dijon mustard.

4 Prepare a grill for indirect medium heat (350° to 450°F).

5 Grill the tenderloin over direct medium heat for 2 minutes a side, 8 minutes total.

6 Move to indirect heat and continue to grill until the internal temperature of the tenderloin reads 145°F with an instant-read thermometer, approximately 12 to 15 minutes. Baste with the glaze every few minutes.

7 Remove the meat from the grill, tent with aluminum foil, and allow it to rest for 5 minutes. Slice into 1-inch pieces and serve.

PLANKED PORK CHOPS
WITH CIDER REDUCTION

★ **SERVES 2**

★ **INGREDIENTS**

2 bone-in pork chops, approximately 1-inch thick

½ teaspoon paprika

½ teaspoon kosher salt

½ teaspoon freshly cracked black pepper

1 apple, sliced into ¼-inch sections

2 bunches fresh sage, chopped

1 12-ounce hard cider

1 teaspoon apple cider vinegar

★ **EQUIPMENT**

Cedar grilling plank, soaked in water for 30 minutes

Aluminum foil

★ **BEER PAIRING**

Weizenbock

Chops and steaks benefit from a sear for flavor, as the most flavor comes from the sear and its browning action on the grates. Here, I'm substituting the sear with a wood plank for an entirely different flavor, smoldering cedar. Wood grilling planks are adaptable to so many different foods on the grill, and I love the use here. Make sure the plank is heated first so that it begins to smolder. This is key and maximizes the amount of time the pork chop comes in contact with the smoke. This recipe also moves the plank from direct to indirect heat. If the plank starts to burn too much over direct heat, move it to indirect sooner, and lengthen your cooking time to hit the target temperature.

1   Prepare a grill for indirect medium heat (350° to 450°F).

2   Grill one side of the plank over direct medium heat until the plank starts to smolder, about 1 to 2 minutes.

3   Season the pork chops with paprika, salt, and pepper. Place the pork chops on the burned side of the plank and top with apple sections and sage.

4   In a small saucepan, heat the cider and cider vinegar until boiling. Lower the heat to simmer and reduce the liquid by half.

5   Grill the plank over direct medium heat for approximately 10 minutes. Move to indirect heat and continue to grill until the internal temperature of the pork reads 145°F with an instant-read thermometer, approximately 35 to 40 minutes more. Brush with the cider glaze every 5 minutes.

6   Remove from the grill, loosely tent with aluminum foil, and allow to rest 5 minutes.

CAROLINA PORK SLIDERS
WITH COLESLAW

I savor my hamburgers, and I enjoy an excellent slider—but I love a pork tenderloin slider. First, they are unexpectedly different. With the first tender bite of succulent pork, it's immediately apparent it's not a hamburger, even though it's nestled in a bun . Second, they are so easy to grill. Unlike a burger made with ground meat, a pork tenderloin slider is simply a pork tenderloin, cut into 1-inch slices to make sliders. There are no worries here about juggling a handful of burgers across the grate to make sure each one cooks correctly. With a pork tenderloin slider, once the tenderloin cooks, they are all done. While Dijon mustard works wonderfully as a glaze, giving an aggressive, vibrant tang to the pork, the real hero is the slaw. It's a perfect complement to the glazed tenderloin. No need for any additional condiments, the slaw topping is all these sliders need. Be sure to make the slaw ahead of time to allow the flavors to meld, and then try not to eat it all before grilling the pork!

★ **SERVES 4**

★ **INGREDIENTS**

FOR THE SLAW

¼ cup extra-virgin olive oil

¼ cup apple cider vinegar

1 teaspoon sugar

1 shallot, minced

¼ teaspoon kosher salt

⅛ teaspoon freshly cracked black pepper

1 8-ounce package coleslaw mix

3 tablespoons Dijon mustard

2 cloves garlic, minced

1 teaspoon kosher salt

½ teaspoon freshly cracked black pepper

1 pork tenderloin

8 slider buns

★ **BEER PAIRING**

Bière de Garde

1. In a medium bowl, whisk together the oil, vinegar, sugar, shallots, salt, and pepper. Stir in the coleslaw mix. Cover and refrigerate.

2. In a small bowl, combine the mustard, garlic, salt, and pepper.

3. Brush the tenderloin with the mustard mixture.

4. Prepare a grill for indirect medium heat (350° to 450°F).

5. Grill the tenderloin over indirect heat until the internal temperature reads 145°F with an instant-read thermometer, approximately 25 to 35 minutes.

6. Remove pork from the grill and cut into 1-inch slices.

7. Grill the buns cut-side down, over direct heat until marked, approximately 1 minute.

8. Load each bun with a tenderloin slice and top with coleslaw. Serve.

BEER BRATS

★ **SERVES 5**

★ **INGREDIENTS**

5 bratwurst sausages

2 12-ounce Märzen beers

2 cups sauerkraut, drained, reserving ½ cup liquid

Top-sliced hot dog buns

5 dill pickles, sliced lengthwise

Spicy brown mustard

★ **EQUIPMENT**

Foil pan

Cast-iron skillet

★ **BEER PAIRING**

Imperial Porter

While a sausage's delicious ratio of meat to fat makes for near-perfect eating, it can also set the stage for a grilling disaster if you are not careful. Just a pinprick to a sausage's casing can produce a stream of fat just waiting to catch fire as it plunges to the coals below. To avoid this, and to guarantee perfectly grilled sausages, start the sausages on the grate to get a nice sear, then move them to a beer bath to finish cooking. Not only does beer prevent flare-ups and fires from the fat, but it also adds even more flavor as the sausages gently simmer in the pan.

1 Prepare a grill with a two-zone fire for indirect medium heat (350° to 450°F).

2 Grill the brats over direct heat for 2 minutes, flipping once.

3 Fill a foil pan with the beer then add the brats to the beer bath.

4 Grill over indirect medium heat, flipping once, for 12 to 15 minutes, or until the internal temperature of the brats reads 145°F with an instant-read thermometer.

5 Place the sauerkraut in a small cast-iron skillet and grill over direct heat for 5 minutes or until heated through.

6 Grill the inside of the buns over direct heat for 30 seconds or until marked.

7 Grill the sliced side of the pickles over direct heat for 2 minutes, flipping once.

8 Load a bun with sauerkraut and a brat. Top with mustard. Serve with a pickle.

GRILLED
MONTE CRISTO SANDWICHES

I'm not a big sandwich guy, but years ago, I could never get enough of the Monte Cristo sandwich served at a now-bygone local restaurant. The Monte Cristo is a mixture of ham, turkey, and cheese, bathed in an egg wash and fried. Covered in powdered sugar and rounded out with a side of raspberry jam, it was heaven on a plate. At least to me. Years after the restaurant closed, I heard someone mention "Monte Cristo" and I knew instantly that I was destined to make a Monte Cristo on the grill. Much like my hazy memories of this extra-special sandwich, my incarnation didn't disappoint. It is cheesy, savory, and sweet as ever. The restaurant may be gone from the area, but my love for this sandwich carries on. I'm glad my memory didn't disappoint.

1   Spread the mustard across two slices of bread. Top each slice of bread with two slices of turkey, ham, Gouda, and Swiss.

2   Spread Dijon mustard across two more slices of bread and place them mustard-side-down on the previous stacks. Top each with two slices of turkey, ham, Gouda, and Swiss.

3   Spread mustard across two more slices of bread and place them mustard-side-down on the stacks. With your hands, smash each stack down.

4   In a medium bowl, beat the eggs and water. Dip all sides of each sandwich in the egg bath. Set aside.

5   Prepare a grill for direct medium heat (350° to 450°F). Preheat a cast-iron skillet on the grill for 15 minutes.

6   Grill the sandwiches in the skillet over direct heat for 10 minutes, flipping once.

7   Remove from the grill. Slice each sandwich in half and sprinkle with powdered sugar. Serve with raspberry jam.

★ **SERVES 2**

★ **INGREDIENTS**
6 slices whole wheat bread
Dijon mustard
8 slices deli-cut roasted turkey
8 slices deli-cut smoked ham
8 slices Gouda cheese
8 slices Swiss cheese
2 eggs
1 teaspoon water
Powdered sugar
Raspberry jam

★ **EQUIPMENT**
Cast-iron skillet

★ **BEER PAIRING**
Hefewezien

CHAPTER 5

SEAFOOD

CEDAR PLANK SALMON

★ **SERVES 4**

★ **INGREDIENTS**

1 salmon fillet, 1½ to 2 pounds

½ teaspoon kosher salt

¼ teaspoon freshly cracked black pepper

½ lemon, sliced

Fresh dill

★ **EQUIPMENT**

Cedar grilling plank, soaked in water for 30 minutes

★ **BEER PAIRING**

Belgian Saison

Grilling salmon on a cedar plank is a quintessential preparation dating back to the Native Americans of the Pacific Northwest, who secured fresh-caught salmon to cedar planks and cooked them next to a fire. While some aficionados still prepare salmon the same way, I prefer using a cedar plank on my grill. I've prepared salmon this way for decades, so it's not surprising to see this method make its way onto restaurant menus. It's a really great way to enjoy salmon, and for the backyard enthusiast, it is an incredibly easy way to grill fish. Be sure to use a food-safe grilling plank and to soak the plank in water for at least 30 minutes before grilling. You can reuse the plank a few times, so be sure not to pitch it when finished with dinner. Once you plank salmon, you will most certainly want that plank to do it again.

1 Prepare a grill for direct medium heat (350° to 450°F).

2 Grill one side of the plank over direct medium heat until the plank starts to smolder, about 1 to 2 minutes.

3 Place the salmon on the burned side of the cedar plank, skin-side down. Season with salt and pepper.

4 Arrange the lemon slices on the flesh followed by several sprigs of fresh drill.

5 Grill over direct heat until the flesh turns opaque, approximately 12 to 15 minutes.

GRILLED SEA BASS
WITH DILL SAUCE

Grilling fish gets a bad rap. Not because it's not good, but because it's perceived to be difficult. When the topic of grilled fish comes up, I am invariably asked, "How do I keep fish from sticking to the grill?" I understand this concern because it still happens to me at times, but I don't want the fear of it to discourage you. Fish is fantastic on the grill, so to pull it off, be sure to preheat the grill and clean the grates thoroughly. The cooked flesh of the fish will release from a cleaned grate, but not from a grate crusted with burnt food. Also, the fish will release from the grate when it's cooked. If you feel a little bit of resistance, wait a minute more and try again. Finally, be sure to oil the fish before putting it on the grate. Better yet, use a fatty fish like this sea bass to ensure success.

1 In a small bowl, combine the sauce ingredients and set aside.

2 Brush the sea bass with olive oil and season with salt and pepper.

3 Prepare a grill for direct medium heat (350° to 450ºF).

4 Starting flesh-side down, grill the fish over direct medium heat until the flesh beings to flake and is cooked through, approximately 10 to 12 minutes, flipping once.

5 Serve with the sauce.

★ **SERVES 3**

★ **INGREDIENTS**
FOR THE SAUCE
½ cup sour cream
2 tablespoons fresh dill, minced
1 teaspoon fresh lemon juice
¼ teaspoon kosher salt

1 sea bass fillet, approximately 1 pound
1 teaspoon extra-virgin olive oil
½ teaspoon kosher salt
¼ teaspoon freshly cracked black pepper

★ **BEER PAIRING**
Lambic

SPICY RUM
SHRIMP SKEWERS

★ **SERVES 4**

★ **INGREDIENTS**

FOR THE MARINADE

2 ounces dark rum

Zest of one lime

2 ounces fresh lime juice

¼ cup chili sauce like sriracha

¼ cup extra-virgin olive oil

1 teaspoon honey

1 teaspoon Dijon mustard

½ teaspoon kosher salt

1 pound (26-30 count) raw shrimp, peeled and deveined,

★ **EQUIPMENT**

One-gallon resealable plastic bag

4 wooden skewers, soaked in water for 30 minutes

★ **BEER PAIRING**

Belgian Pale Ale

When I'm looking to go on a tropical vacation without leaving the house, this is what I grill. These shrimp skewers hit all of the right warm-breeze notes I'm after, starting with the rum and lime juice. Since I often need a "getaway" at the last minute, I always keep a bag of frozen shrimp in the freezer. With the shrimp's fast thaw under cold water and an equally quick marinade in the refrigerator, I can have dinner ready for the grill in under an hour. Shrimp are straightforward to grill, only taking a few minutes on the grate until their flesh becomes opaque, a sure sign of doneness. To make things even simpler, put the shrimp on skewers. It's a lot less work lifting four skewers off the grill than twenty shrimp. Now, where are my hurricane glasses and cocktail umbrellas?

1 In a bowl, whisk together the marinade ingredients. Set aside ¼ cup for basting. Pour the rest into the plastic bag. Add the shrimp. Remove as much as air as possible from the bag, seal, and refrigerate for 30 to 60 minutes.

2 Prepare a grill for direct medium heat (350° to 450°F).

3 Remove the shrimp from the bag and discard the marinade. Place the shrimp on the skewers.

4 Grill the shrimp over direct heat until the flesh turns opaque, flipping once, approximately 4 to 6 minutes. Baste with the reserved marinade in the last two minutes.

HICKORY GRILLED TROUT

★ **SERVES 2**

★ **INGREDIENTS**

1 rainbow trout, approximately 1 pound, cleaned

½ teaspoon kosher salt

¼ teaspoon freshly cracked black pepper

6 lemon slices, approximately ¼ inch thick

1 branch rosemary

1 teaspoon extra-virgin olive oil

★ **EQUIPMENT**

Hickory wood chunks or chips

★ **BEER PAIRING**

Amber Lager

Grilling a whole fish, such as a trout, is about as primitive as it gets. It's also incredibly easy and super satisfying. Keeping the fish whole means the fish's oily skin virtually eliminates the possibility of the fish sticking to the grates. Also, the skin protects the flesh, allowing it to maintain moisture and reducing the chance of its drying out on the grate. Once cooked, remove a fillet from one side of the fish, discard the bone cage, and then remove the remaining fillet. Be sure to save the skin, which is delicious on its own. For success, it all starts with sourcing the freshest fish possible. Look for shiny scales, tight gills, and clear eyes. Grilling a whole fish may seem challenging, but it will end up being your go-to method.

1 With a pair of scissors, remove the fins from the trout. Season the trout with salt and pepper. Stuff the cavity with lemon slices and pieces of rosemary. Brush the skin with olive oil.

2 Prepare a grill for direct medium heat (350° to 450°F).

3 Once at temperature, add 2 or 3 hickory wood chunks to lit briquettes or, on a gas grill, hickory wood chips to a smoker box or foil packet.

4 Grill the trout over direct heat until the flesh flakes and is opaque, approximately 12 to 15 minutes, flipping every 5 minutes.

5 Remove from the grill. Remove the skin and flesh from each side of the trout and serve.

COD KEBABS

When you hear "kebabs," I'm willing to bet fish does not immediately come to mind. Instead, your mind might flash to horror stories of fish sticking to the grill as you watch dinner literally go down in flames. Oh no, not so. I refuse to steer you wrong. Cod, with its dense, thick flesh, is excellent for grilling and perfect for skewering. Kebabs are the perfect opportunity to incorporate great flavor and textures, like the sweet-tart of grilled grape tomatoes and the crunch of panko bread crumbs in this recipe. Be sure to preheat and clean the grill at least 20 minutes ahead of time to prevent the fish from sticking. The kebabs will rotate when the flesh is ready, so don't rush it.

1 Cut the cod into 1-inch cubes

2 Thread alternating pieces of cod and tomatoes on the wooden skewers.

3 Brush the kebabs with olive oil and season with salt and pepper.

4 In a small bowl, combine the bread crumbs and the herbes de Provence

5 Sprinkle the bread crumb mixture over all sides of the kabobs.

6 Preheat the grill for direct medium heat (350° to 450°F). To prevent the fish from sticking, preheat the grill at least 20 minutes and thoroughly clean the grates with a grill brush.

7 Grill the kebabs over direct heat until the cod begins to flake, flipping once, approximately 8 to 10 minutes.

★ **SERVES 4**

★ **INGREDIENTS**
  1 cod fillet, about 1½ to 2 pounds
  12 grape tomatoes
  1 tablespoon extra-virgin olive oil
  ¾ teaspoon kosher salt
  ½ teaspoon freshly cracked black pepper
  ½ cup panko bread crumbs
  1 teaspoon herbes de Provence

★ **EQUIPMENT**
  4 wooden skewers, soaked in water for 30 minutes

★ **BEER PAIRING**
  Altbier

GRILLED SCALLOPS
WITH GREMOLATA

If you have never grilled scallops, you are in for a treat. File these under "Seafood Not Grilled Often Enough." They are so easy to grill and divine to feast upon. Often, scallops are grilled in a pan or on a griddle, but since I enjoy them directly on the grates, I go for the larger sea scallops rather than their smaller siblings, the tiny bay scallops. Taking only a matter of minutes to cook, the scallops are easy to flip and rarely stick, thanks to their oily flesh. Most important, I love the grill marks left behind. These delectable morsels pair beautifully with freshly made Italian gremolata.

1 Over a cutting board, use a microplane to grate lemon zest onto the parsley. Grate the garlic the same way. Using a chef's knife, stir and continue to chop the parsley, lemon zest, and garlic until minced and evenly combined. Transfer to a small bowl.

2 Brush the scallops with olive oil and season with salt and pepper.

3 Prepare a grill for direct medium heat (350º to 450ºF).

4 Grill the scallops over direct heat until firm and opaque, approximately 4 to 6 minutes, flipping once.

5 Top the scallops with gremolata and serve.

★ SERVES 2

★ INGREDIENTS
½ cup Italian parsley, finely chopped
1 lemon
2 cloves garlic
1 pound sea scallops, abductor muscle removed
1 tablespoon extra-virgin olive oil
½ teaspoon kosher salt
¼ teaspoon freshly cracked black pepper

★ EQUIPMENT
Cutting board
Microplane

★ BEER PAIRING
American Wheat

GRILLED LOBSTER TAILS

★ SERVES 2

★ INGREDIENTS

¼ cup unsalted butter, room temperature

1 tablespoon cilantro, chopped

Zest of one lemon

Juice of ½ lemon

2 lobster tails, 6 to 8 ounces each

Extra-virgin olive oil

Kosher salt

Freshly cracked black pepper

★ BEER PAIRING

Wheat Wine Ale

Lobster is decadent, and when ordered out at a restaurant, often expensive. Instead, I love to treat myself to grilled lobster at home. While not quite as tasty as their cold-water cousins, warm-water lobsters are cheaper and can be found at most grocery stores. Lobster tails are easy to cook and are great for taking on the grill's flavors. Whether they serve as the "surf" for your turf, a meal on their own, or a surprise appetizer for guests, lobster tails grilled at home are easily better than lobster boiled at a restaurant, especially when served with a zesty herb compound butter. You may never order lobster out again.

1   In a small bowl, combine the butter, cilantro, lemon zest, and lemon juice. Set aside.

2   With a pair of scissors, remove the swimmerets, the small tail appendages on the underside of the lobster tail.

3   Cut the top of the shell starting at the exposed flesh portion and stopping just short of the tail fins. With a knife, split the meat along the same line, but do not cut through the lower membrane. Open the tail like a book to expose the flesh.

4   Prepare a grill for direct medium heat (350° to 450°F).

5   Brush the lobster flesh with olive oil and season with salt and pepper.

6   Grill the lobster tails over direct heat, flesh-side-down, for 5 minutes. Flip the lobster tails and continue to grill until the flesh turns opaque, approximately 5 to 7 minutes more. Brush with half the butter during the last few minutes of grilling. Serve with the remaining butter.

WALLEYE TACOS
WITH SALSA VERDE

Fish tacos rock. What more can I say? Love is not strong enough of a word to express my passion for fish tacos. In fact, I need multiple words, like "absolutely treasure," "strongly adore," or "man, these are just the best ever." Quite simply, I never met a fish taco I didn't like. Through the years, I've prepared them countless ways, with different fish species, multiple toppings, and varied cheeses. But basically, the best tacos use the freshest fish. Here I've used walleye, but mahi-mahi, haddock, and cod are all great alternatives. For salsa, I go with salsa verde with its fresh, tart tomatillo base. Much like the choice of fish, the salsa options are endless. Whatever you do, don't forget the cheese. Salty and crumbly cotija is the perfect finish for one of my favorite meals.

1 Brush the walleye with olive oil and season with salt and pepper.

2 Prepare a grill for direct medium heat (350° to 450°F). To prevent the fish from sticking, preheat the grill at least 20 minutes and thoroughly clean the grates with a grill brush.

3 Grill the walleye over direct heat for 5 minutes. If the fish does not release from the grates, cook a minute longer. Flip the walleye and cook until the flesh begins to flake, approximately 2 to 3 minutes.

4 Grill the tortillas over direct medium heat for 1 minute, flipping once.

5 Evenly divide the fish, salsa verde, cheese, and cilantro among the tacos. Top with fresh lime juice.

★ **SERVES 2**

★ **INGREDIENTS**

1 walleye fillet, about ½ pound

1 teaspoon extra-virgin olive oil

¼ teaspoon kosher salt

⅛ teaspoon freshly cracked black pepper

4 8-inch flour tortillas

¾ cup store-bought salsa verde

½ cup cotija cheese

2 tablespoons freshly chopped cilantro

1 lime, sliced into wedges

★ **BEER PAIRING**
Spiced Beer

CHAPTER 6

SIDES

GRILLED TOMATOES

★ INGREDIENTS
  4 vine-ripened tomatoes
  1 tablespoon extra-virgin olive oil
  1 teaspoon kosher salt
  2 tablespoons fresh basil, chopped

★ BEER PAIRING
  Gose

I love this recipe for two reasons. First, it's about as easy as it gets. In fact, it is funny how the simplest things to hit the grill are often the best. It might look complicated or involved, but it's not. Second, it just looks great and you want to take a bite. Interestingly, I grew up not liking tomatoes. Sure, if they were heavily seasoned in salsa or a sauce, yes. But a straight raw tomato? No thanks, freak. Fast forward decades later and here I am eating only a slightly cooked tomato with a slight bit of seasoning and I can't get enough. These tomatoes are at their best on warm summer nights fresh off the vine and straight to the grill.

1 Place the tomatoes on their sides and cut them into ½ inch-thick slices, discarding the top and bottom.

2 Brush both sides of the tomato slices with olive oil and season with kosher salt.

3 Prepare a grill for direct medium heat (350° to 450°F).

4 Grill the tomato slices over direct heat for approximately 3 to 4 minutes, flipping once.

5 Remove from the grill and top with fresh basil.

LEMON-PEPPER ASPARAGUS

I have two thoughts on asparagus: they are fantastic on the grill, and they need to use the buddy system, as I invariably lose a few between the grates. I guarantee if we were to go clean my firebox right now, I'd find at least two incinerated asparagus spears, and that's on a good day. While I never return to the kitchen with the same number of asparagus I left with, they are excellent grilled and worth the casualties. Asparagus is best when cooked hot and fast, and depending on their size, need no more than 6 minutes on the grill. The finishing touch of freshly squeezed lemon juice makes the asparagus shine, at least those that make it to the serving platter.

★ **SERVES 4**

★ **INGREDIENTS**

1 bunch asparagus, about 15 to 20 spears

1 tablespoon extra-virgin olive oil

1 teaspoon lemon pepper

½ teaspoon kosher salt

½ lemon

★ **BEER PAIRING**

Black Ale

1 Snap off the fibrous bottom of the asparagus stalk with your fingers. In a shallow bowl, toss the asparagus with olive oil and then the lemon pepper and salt.

2 Prepare a grill for direct medium-high heat (400° to 450°F).

3 Grill the asparagus over direct heat for 6 to 8 minutes until well marked, approximately 6 to 8 minutes, rotating several times.

4 Remove to a serving platter. Drizzle with squeezed lemon juice. Serve.

GRILLED PINEAPPLE SALSA

★ SERVES 4

★ INGREDIENTS

1½ pounds roma tomatoes, halved

2 jalapeños, halved, seeds and ribs removed

½ red onion, peeled and quartered

1-inch slice of a fresh pineapple, peeled and cored

2 cloves garlic

1 tablespoon extra-virgin olive oil

2 tablespoons fresh cilantro, chopped

2 limes, juiced

½ teaspoon kosher salt

★ EQUIPMENT

Perforated grill pan

Blender or food processor

★ BEER PAIRING

Golden Ale

I sometimes purchase store-bought salsa out of sheer laziness. This is doubly true in the summer months, when local produce is bountiful. But the fact is, salsa is best made at home. It's so easy to prepare that it's borderline criminal if you don't. For Grilled Pinapple Salsa, aside from a grill, obviously, you will need two additional tools: a perforated grill pan and a blender. The grill pan is a must to contain the ingredients. With the smaller openings, it is impossible to lose anything through the larger spaces of the grates. The blender or food processor is used to mix everything together. If you prefer a chunkier salsa, reduce the blending. If you want an evenly combined and finer salsa, blend longer. The caramelization on the grilled pineapple puts this salsa over the top. You will see why I think it is the best, and you'll kiss those jars goodbye.

1 Place the tomatoes, jalapeños, onion, and pineapple in a large bowl and toss with the olive oil.

2 Prepare a grill for direct medium-high heat (400° to 450°F). Preheat a grill pan for at least 15 minutes.

3 Grill the tomatoes, jalapeños, onion, and pineapple on the grill pan over direct heat until marked, approximately 10 to 12 minutes, flipping once. Add the garlic cloves during the last 2 minutes.

4 Remove the ingredients from the grill and place them in a food processor or blender. Add cilantro, lime juice, and salt. Pulse until combined to desired consistency.

GRILLED FRIES

I love a good French fry, but frying anything at home can be a legit pain. As a worthy substitute, I get my fry kick on the grill. A grilled potato is always satisfying, but to emulate the fast frying action of hot oil, I parboil the potatoes before grilling. This process cooks the inside of the potato so the fry can spend less time on the grill over high heat. My second move is to add baking soda to help the fries brown quickly. Although it is not a requirement, I suggest using a perforated grill pan. While you still need to rotate the fries through their cooking time, a pan makes it easier to move the fries on and off the grill. Plus, the pan reduces the odds of losing a fry through the grill grates' wide spaces.

★ **SERVES 2**

★ **INGREDIENTS**

2 russet potatoes

1 teaspoon kosher salt

½ teaspoon freshly cracked black pepper

½ teaspoon onion powder

½ teaspoon baking soda

2 tablespoons extra-virgin olive oil

★ **EQUIPMENT**

Perforated grill pan

★ **BEER PAIRING**

Irish Red

5 Cut the potatoes into ½-inch wide fries. Place the potato slices in a pot of boiling water and parboil for 3 minutes. Remove them from the pot and cool the potatoes in a bowl of ice water to stop them from cooking.

6 Prepare a grill for direct medium-high heat (400° to 450°F). Preheat the grill pan for at least 15 minutes.

7 Remove the potatoes from the ice bath and place them on a paper towel-lined sheet pan. Using additional paper towels, blot them dry.

8 Discard the paper towels and toss the potatoes with the salt, pepper, onion powder, baking soda, and olive oil.

9 Grill the potatoes on the grill pan over direct medium-high heat for 7 minutes, flipping once.

SMOKED
MACARONI AND CHEESE

★ **INGREDIENTS**

1 pound macaroni elbows

4 tablespoons unsalted butter

½ cup all-purpose flour

2 cups whole milk

1½ pounds cheddar cheese, shredded

1 teaspoon ground mustard

½ pound Gruyère cheese, shredded

1 tablespoon unsalted butter

1 jalapeño, halved and sliced

★ **EQUIPMENT**

Cast-iron skillet

Hickory wood chunks or chips

★ **BEER PAIRING**

Rye Beer

In my never-ending quest to get everyone out of the kitchen and out by the grill, I would be completely fine if it were taken in gradual steps. For instance, if your go-to mac and cheese comes from a blue box, keep making it as usual, but have it spend some time on the grill the next time you make it. Can you taste the difference? It's amazing what a little smoke can do. But now it's time to ditch the box and make Smoked Macaroni and Cheese from scratch. I get that squeezing gelatinous cheese from a foil pouch is easy, but making a roux and adding the cheese of your choosing is really not *that* much harder. If the grill is already set up for smoking BBQ, it's easy to make a little space on the grate for Smoked Macaroni and Cheese. Pretty soon, the only reason to be in the kitchen is to wash the dishes.

1   Cook the macaroni until it is al dente, about one minute less than package directions.

2   On the stovetop, in a large skillet over medium heat, melt the butter. Add the flour to the butter and whisk constantly until combined and fragrant, about one minute.

3   Raise the temperature of the skillet to medium-high and slowly add the milk while whisking. Continue to whisk until the sauce thickens and coats the back of a spoon, about 4 to 5 minutes.

4   Reduce the heat to low. Stir in the cheddar cheese until the cheese melts. Stir in the ground mustard.

5   In a large bowl, combine the macaroni with the cheese sauce. Stir in the Gruyère.

6   Coat the bottom of a large cast-iron skillet with the tablespoon of unsalted butter. Add the macaroni and cheese to the skillet and top with jalapeño slices.

7   Prepare a grill for indirect medium heat (350° to 450°F). Once at temperature, add a hickory wood chunk to lit briquettes or, on a gas grill, hickory wood chips to a smoker box or foil packet.

8   Grill the macaroni and cheese over indirect heat until it's heated through and the top is golden brown, approximately 30 to 40 minutes.

SALSA VERDE TWICE-BAKED
SWEET POTATOES

As a fan of a good twice-baked potato, it seemed only natural that I would use the same cooking process for its cousin, the sweet potato. I guess it's the name, but somehow sweet potatoes always seem to end up with sugar added to them. At some point, they leave the bounds of a healthy vegetable and head directly toward dessert on a magical marshmallow sleigh. I prefer a different road. Salsa verde, whether homemade or store-bought, is the perfect companion for grilled sweet potatoes, giving them a tangy kick. Top them off with the ideal melting cheese, queso Chihuahua, and these sweet potatoes are almost a meal unto themselves, and the farthest thing from dessert.

★ **SERVES 4**

★ **INGREDIENTS**
2 medium sweet potatoes
1 teaspoon extra-virgin olive oil
¼ cup milk
½ teaspoon chili powder
¼ cup salsa verde
½ cup grated queso Chihuahua
1 green onion, sliced

★ **BEER PAIRING**
Pumpkin Beer

1   Prepare a grill for indirect medium heat (350° to 450°F).

2   Brush the potatoes with olive oil. Grill over indirect medium heat until soft, approximately 60 to 75 minutes.

3   Slice the potatoes in half and scoop out the middle, leaving approximately ¼ inch of flesh around the skin.

4   In a medium bowl, mash the removed potato with milk, chili powder, and salsa verde.

5   Fill the halved potatoes with the mashed filling. Top each with the cheese and green onion.

6   Grill the potato halves over indirect medium heat until the cheese has melted and the potatos are heated through, approximately 15 minutes.

GRILLED ZUCCHINI

★ **SERVES 4**

★ **INGREDIENTS**

2 zucchini

Extra-virgin olive oil

½ teaspoon kosher salt

½ teaspoon dried oregano

¼ teaspoon freshly cracked black pepper

★ **BEER PAIRING**

Session Beer

When I started my grilling journey, one of the first vegetables I routinely dropped on the grates was zucchini. Interestingly, this was a vegetable I never had growing up, so it might explain my late-in-life interest. Whether cut into planks, wedges, or scooped out and stuffed, grilled zucchini are a delectable, healthy treat. My dad says he is not a fan, but I'm pretty sure I've watched him sneak a few when I've served them at family dinners. They take just a few minutes to grill and need just a touch of seasoning. If you are looking for variety, consider adding summer squash to the mix, which is very similar in taste and grills up the same.

1 Slice the zucchini lengthwise, into ¼-inch-thick planks.

2 Brush the zucchini with olive oil and season with salt, oregano, and black pepper.

3 Prepare the grill for direct medium heat (350° to 450°F).

4 Grill the zucchini over direct heat for 6 minutes, flipping once.

PLANKED TWICE-BAKED
MASHED POTATOES

What happens when you're in your kitchen, staring at a pot of mashed potatoes, and happen to be holding a grilling plank? Well, you may just stumble into inventing twice-baked magic. If you love twice-baked potatoes, this is an easier way to prepare them for a large group. The smoldering plank adds its sweet gift of smoke to the towering pile of spuds and is easier to manage than individual potatoes. I'm all about a side dish that tastes amazing and makes my dinner process easier, so I love the added benefit that these can be partially prepared in advance and then grilled when needed.

1 Fill a large pot with water and bring to a boil. Add the potatoes. Return the water to a boil and cook until the potatoes are easily pierced with a knife, approximately 10 to 12 minutes.

2 Drain the potatoes in a colander and wipe the pot dry. Add the butter and the boiled potatoes to the pot. Mash the potatoes and butter together while adding in the milk. Stir in the sour cream, garlic, rosemary, salt, and pepper. Can be made a day in advance.

3 Prepare a grill for indirect medium heat (350° to 450°F).

4 Grill one side of the plank over direct medium heat until the plank starts to smolder, about 1 to 2 minutes.

5 Load the center of the burnt side of the grilling plank with mashed potatoes. Top with cheese and onion.

6 Grill over direct heat for 10 minutes, then move to indirect heat and continue to grill until the potatoes are heated through, approximately 20 minutes more, or longer if potatoes were made in advance.

★ **SERVES 4**

★ **INGREDIENTS**

4 medium russet potatoes, cubed, with skin on

½ cup unsalted butter

½ cup milk

2 tablespoons sour cream

3 cloves garlic, minced

2 tablespoons fresh rosemary, minced

½ teaspoon kosher salt

¼ teaspoon freshly cracked black pepper

⅓ cup shredded cheddar cheese

1 green onion, thinly sliced

★ **EQUIPMENT**

Cedar grilling plank, soaked in water for 30 minutes

★ **BEER PAIRING**

Old Ale

HASSELBACK POTATOES

★ **SERVES 2**

★ **INGREDIENTS**
2 large russet potatoes

FOR THE RUB
½ teaspoon kosher salt
½ teaspoon onion powder
¼ teaspoon freshly cracked
black pepper

1 tablespoon extra-virgin olive oil
2 tablespoons unsalted butter,
quartered
¼ cup shredded cheddar cheese
1 tablespoon green chilis, diced

★ **EQUIPMENT**
Chopsticks or wooden spoons

★ **BEER PAIRING**
Bohemian Pilsner

The hasselback potato, not to be confused with the Hasselhoff potato, is another excellent way of preparing a russet for the grill. Making thin, perpendicular slices along the potato increases the surface area, exposing the inside to heat during the cooking process. The cuts don't go all the way through the potato; the base of the potato acts like a spine. While a hasselback cooks faster than a whole potato, an added plus, my favorite highlight is the resulting crispy potato slices. Think of it almost like a row of thick-cut potato chips. Toward the cook's end, I add in butter, chilis, and cheese to bring it all together. It's a unique and delicious presentation I go to again and again.

1   Cut a small slice off the long side of each potato so that it lies flat on a cutting board.

2   Place chopsticks or wooden spoons along each long side of the potato. Starting ½ inch from one end of the potato, make a vertical cut into the potato every ¼ inch until reaching ½ inch from the opposite end. The chopsticks or wooden spoons will keep the knife from cutting all of the way through the potato.

3   In a small bowl, combine the salt, onion powder, and pepper. Brush each potato with olive oil and season with the rub, trying to get in between the potato slices.

4   Preheat a grill for indirect medium-high heat (400° to 450°F).

5   Grill the potatoes over indirect heat until cooked through and browned, approximately 45 minutes. During the last 5 minutes, top the potatoes with butter. Once the butter melts, top with cheese and chilis. Remove the potatoes from the grill when the cheese has melted.

GRILLED CAESAR SALAD

If you want to watch your friends' heads spin, tell them you're grilling salad for dinner. My announcement was met with wandering eyes, trying to find out where I had been hit in the head. It might sound crazy, but grilled lettuce—specifically romaine—is a delicious treat. Halving a romaine heart and grilling each side over a hot fire for a few minutes transforms both the taste and texture of this water-rich green. I'm open to any number of dressings and toppings, but I always gravitate toward my favorite: Caesar. I'm perfectly fine with a quality store-bought dressing, but I insist on freshly grated Parmigiano-Reggiano, and the ever-so-divisive anchovies. I strongly feel they are a necessary addition. No judging! Surprise your guests next time, and instead of taking it to the table, take the salad to the grill.

★ **SERVES 2**

★ **INGREDIENTS**
  1 head romaine lettuce
  ½ teaspoon kosher salt
  ¼ teaspoon freshly cracked black pepper
  ¼ cup grated Parmigiano-Reggiano cheese
  ¼ cup store-bought Caesar dressing
  Croutons
  2 anchovy fillets, optional

★ **BEER PAIRING**
  Belgian Blonde Ale

1 Slice the romaine head in half lengthwise. Season with salt and pepper.

2 Prepare a grill for direct medium heat (350° to 450°F).

3 Grill the romaine halves over direct heat until marked, approximately 4 minutes, flipping once.

4 Top with cheese, dressing, croutons, and anchovy fillets.

AU GRATIN POTATOES

★ SERVES 4

★ INGREDIENTS

3 large russet potatoes, sliced thin

2 cups heavy cream

4 fresh thyme sprigs

3 cloves garlic

1½ cups Parmigiano-Reggiano cheese, grated

½ teaspoon kosher salt

¼ teaspoon freshly cracked black pepper

★ EQUIPMENT

Large cast-iron skillet

★ BEER PAIRING

Belgian Lambic

Potatoes never get old. They go with just about any beer style and are endlessly adaptable to the grill, and everyone loves them. Au gratin potatoes, typically prepared in a dish under a broiler for a beautiful cheesy crust, are even better on the grill. They take on the wonderful trademark crust and absorb the swirling flavors of BBQ. If you want to ramp up the dish's smokiness, place a wood chunk directly on the grate over direct heat.

1   In a large bowl, combine all of the ingredients and then spread them evenly in the bottom of a cast-iron skillet.

2   Prepare a grill for indirect medium-heat (350° to 450°F).

3   Grill the potatoes over indirect medium heat until tender and browned, approximately 35 to 45 minutes.

4   Remove and serve.

CHAPTER 7

PIZZA

GRILLED
MARGHERITA PIZZA

★ **SERVES 2**

★ **INGREDIENTS**
⅔ cup warm water
1 packet active dry yeast
½ teaspoon sugar
¼ cup extra-virgin olive oil
½ teaspoon kosher salt
2 cups bread flour
⅔ cup pizza sauce
2 roma tomatoes, sliced
1 bunch fresh basil, coarsely chopped
½ cup fresh mozzarella, shredded

★ **EQUIPMENT**
Food processor
Wax paper

★ **BEER PAIRING**
India Pale Lager

NOTE: This recipe calls for the use of a food processor to make the dough. It is an easy and foolproof method. If you don't have a food processor, you can easily substitute a stand mixer or your hands. But seriously, get a food processor.

Years ago, I thought about putting in a pizza oven. I've since pushed the thought aside upon realizing I already have the best pizza over there is, and it's sitting in my backyard. If you have never grilled pizza before, don't let it intimidate you. Whether you grill on the grates, or on a stone, or if you prefer homemade dough to store-bought, it's all doable, and all of these recipes can be mixed and matched. The classic Margherita pizza is one of my favorites. Here, the dough is made from scratch and grilled on the grates. It's wonderfully simple and utterly delicious.

1   Combine water, yeast, and sugar in the bowl of a food processor equipped with a dough blade and allow it to proof, approximately 5 minutes.

2   Add ¼ cup olive oil, salt, and flour to the food processor and pulse until the dough comes off the sides and forms a ball, approximately 3 to 5 minutes.

3   Place the dough on a clean, lightly floured surface. Work it into a smooth, round ball. Place the dough ball in a large, lightly oiled bowl; cover with a clean cloth and allow the dough to rise until doubled in size, about 1 hour.

4   Return the dough to the counter and reform into a ball. Cover with a towel.

5   Prepare the grill for indirect medium-high heat (400° to 450°F).

6   Cut the dough ball in half and work each half into a circle measuring approximately 8 inches in diameter, using either a rolling pin or your hands.

7   Place the dough on wax paper and lightly brush each side with olive oil. Score the dough with a fork.

8   Grill the pizza dough over direct heat until the dough begins to set up and is marked by the grill, approximately 1 to 2 minutes.

9   Return the pizza dough to the wax paper, grilled side up.

10 Top the pizzas with sauce, tomatoes, basil, and cheese.

11 Grill the first pizza over indirect heat with the lid down for 5 to 6 minutes or until the dough is cooked. Repeat with the second pizza.

SAUSAGE, HAM, AND ROASTED RED PEPPER PIZZA

The most authentic grilled pizza makes use of a pizza stone as an attempt to replicate the bottom of a ceramic pizza oven. Years ago, my first pizza stone was an actual 16-inch square ceramic tile purchased from a big box hardware store. It had a limited life, but it worked like a charm, until it didn't. Today, durable grilling stones are readily available and are more suited for the task. The key to using a stone is indirect fire and a long grill preheat. Too much heat directly below the stone is a ticket to a burnt crust. The bottom cooks way before the toppings have a chance. However, a lot of heat around the stone, coupled with that long preheat, sets up the grill for a perfectly cooked and beautifully blistered pizza.

1 Combine water, yeast, and sugar in the bowl of a food processor equipped with a dough blade and allow it to proof, approximately 5 minutes.

2 Add ¼ cup olive oil, salt, and flour to the food processor and pulse until the dough comes off the sides and forms a ball, approximately 3 to 5 minutes.

3 Place the dough on a clean, lightly floured surface. Work it into a smooth, round ball. Place the dough ball in a large, lightly oiled bowl; cover with a clean cloth and allow the dough to rise until doubled in size, about 1 hour.

4 Return the dough to the counter and reform into a ball. Cover with a towel.

5 Prepare the grill for indirect high heat (450° to 550°F). Preheat the pizza stone over indirect heat for at least 15 minutes.

6 Cut the dough ball in half and work each half into a circle measuring approximately 8 inches in diameter, using either a rolling pin or your hands.

7 Score the dough with a fork.

8 Sprinkle cornmeal on the countertop. Place the pizza dough on the cornmeal and top each dough round with sauce, ham, sausage, peppers, and cheese.

9 Sprinkle more cornmeal on the peel and transfer one pizza from the countertop to the pizza stone.

10 Grill the pizza with the lid down for 5 to 7 minutes or until the dough is cooked. Repeat with the second pizza.

★ **SERVES 4**

★ **INGREDIENTS**
⅔ cup warm water
1 packet active dry yeast
½ teaspoon sugar
¼ cup extra-virgin olive oil
½ teaspoon kosher salt
2 cups bread flour
Cornmeal
⅔ cup pizza sauce
1 cup diced ham
1 cup cooked pork sausage
½ cup low-moisture mozzarella cheese, shredded
1 roasted red pepper, diced

★ **EQUIPMENT**
Food processor
Pizza stone
Pizza peel

★ **BEER PAIRING**
Scottish Ale

BBQ PULLED PORK PIZZA

I'm always looking for ways to use leftover pulled pork. I've included a recipe for stuffed peppers and mentioned quesadillas, tacos, and nachos, but one of my favorite uses is pizza. Swapping out the tomato sauce for BBQ sauce and opting for pepper jack cheese over mozzarella is transformational. Even though this recipe calls for homemade dough, it is just as easy to substitute frozen store-bought dough, or better yet, fresh store-bought dough if you can find it. The only guideline for grilled pizza is the cooking process. Everything else is up for interpretation and experimentation. Oh, and if this is a last-minute meal, the toppings are whatever is in the fridge. I guarantee it will still be great.

1 Combine water, yeast, and sugar in the bowl of a food processor equipped with a dough blade and allow it to proof, approximately 5 minutes.

2 Add ¼ cup olive oil, salt, and flour to the food processor and pulse until the dough comes off the sides and forms a ball, approximately 3 to 5 minutes.

3 Place the dough on a clean, lightly floured surface. Work it into a smooth, round ball. Place the dough ball in a large, lightly oiled bowl; cover with a clean cloth and allow the dough to rise until doubled in size, about 1 hour.

4 Return the dough to the counter and reform into a ball. Cover with a towel.

5 Prepare the grill for indirect high heat (450° to 550°F). Preheat the pizza stone over indirect heat for at least 15 minutes.

6 Cut the dough ball in half and work each half into a circle measuring approximately 8 inches in diameter, using either a rolling pin or your hands.

7 Score the dough with a fork.

8 Sprinkle cornmeal on the countertop. Place the pizza dough on the cornmeal and top each with sauce, pork, cheese, and chilis.

9 Sprinkle more cornmeal on the peel and transfer the first pizza from the countertop to the pizza stone.

10 Grill the pizza with the lid down for 5 to 7 minutes or until the dough is cooked. Repeat with the second pizza.

★ **SERVES 4**

★ **INGREDIENTS**
⅔ cup warm water
1 packet active dry yeast
½ teaspoon sugar
¼ cup extra-virgin olive oil
½ teaspoon kosher salt
2 cups bread flour
Cornmeal
⅓ cup BBQ sauce
1 cup pulled pork
½ cup pepper jack cheese, shredded
2 tablespoons green chilis, diced

★ **EQUIPMENT**
Food processor
Pizza stone
Pizza peel

★ **BEER PAIRING**
Brett

SMOKED SAUSAGE
GRILLED CALZONE

★ **SERVES 2**

★ **INGREDIENTS**

⅔ cup warm water

1 packet active dry yeast

½ teaspoon sugar

¼ cup extra-virgin olive oil

½ teaspoon kosher salt

2 cups bread flour

⅔ cup pizza sauce

¼ cup chopped yellow onion

½ red bell pepper, chopped

½ green bell pepper, chopped

1 cooked kielbasa sausage, chopped

½ cup low-moisture mozzarella cheese, shredded

1 teaspoon dried oregano

1 egg, beaten

2 tablespoons Parmigiano-Reggiano cheese, grated

Cornmeal

★ **EQUIPMENT**

Food processor

Pizza stone

Pizza peel

★ **BEER PAIRING**

Brown Porter

Lately, I've grilled fewer pizzas and more calzones. When I was in college at Purdue University, we lived on stuffed breadsticks from a local pizzeria. A stuffed breadstick is the Midwest term for a calzone: dough loaded with sauce, cheese, and a meat filling. If you are new to a stone and pizza peel, the calzone is a little more forgiving. This might be an excellent place to hone your grilled pizza skills even if you aren't grilling a traditional pizza. Join me on my sentimental journey and hit the pizza pause button. This calzone is worth it.

---

1 Combine water, yeast, and sugar in the bowl of a food processor equipped with a dough blade and allow it to proof, approximately 5 minutes.

2 Add ¼ cup olive oil, salt, and flour to the food processor and pulse until the dough comes off the sides and forms a ball, approximately 3 to 5 minutes.

3 Place the dough on a clean, lightly floured surface. Work it into a smooth, round ball. Place the dough ball in a large, lightly oiled bowl; cover with a clean cloth and allow the dough to rise until doubled in size, about 1 hour.

4 Return the dough to the counter and reform into a ball. Cover with a towel.

5 Prepare the grill for indirect medium heat (350° to 450°F). Preheat the pizza stone over indirect heat for at least 15 minutes.

6 Using either a rolling pin or your hands, work the dough into a circle measuring approximately 16 inches in diameter.

7 Spread pizza sauce on one half of the circle, leaving about 1 inch of space from the outer edge. Top the sauce evenly with the onion, peppers, sausage, cheese, and oregano.

8 Fold the dough over and seal the edge with your fingers.

9 Brush the top with egg. With a sharp knife, slice three evenly spaced slits on the top of the calzone. Top with freshly grated Parmigiano-Reggiano cheese.

10 Sprinkle cornmeal on the peel and then, using the peel, transfer the dough from the countertop to the pizza stone on the grill.

11 Cook until the dough begins to brown and is cooked through, approximately 15 to 20 minutes.

SAUERKRAUT AND SAUSAGE
PIZZA

Don't let the word "sauerkraut" cross this pizza recipe off your "make now" list. Everyone loves a traditional pizza, but some of my most memorable pizzas have been several times removed from the norm. Just break out your lederhosen, imagine yourself drinking a liter of beer to celebrate Oktoberfest, and pretty soon I'll have you convinced of the deliciousness that is sauerkraut on pizza. Kielbasa and sauerkraut are a classic combination and work well as pizza toppings. One of the highlights of grilling pizzas at home is experimentation. I hope this recipe challenges you to think of other nontraditional pizza toppings. There are a lot out there.

★ **SERVES 4**

★ **INGREDIENTS**
⅔ cup warm water
1 packet active dry yeast
½ teaspoon sugar
¼ cup extra-virgin olive oil
½ teaspoon kosher salt
2 cups bread flour
Cornmeal
⅓ cup pizza sauce
1 cup sauerkraut, drained
1 cup cooked kielbasa sausage, chopped
½ cup low-moisture mozzarella cheese, shredded

★ **EQUIPMENT**
Food processor
Pizza stone
Pizza peel

★ **BEER PAIRING**
Robust Porter

1   Combine water, yeast, and sugar in the bowl of a food processor equipped with a dough blade and allow it to proof, approximately 5 minutes.

2   Add ¼ cup olive oil, salt, and flour to the food processor and pulse until the dough comes off the sides and forms a ball, approximately 3 to 5 minutes.

3   Place the dough on a clean, lightly floured surface. Work it into a smooth, round ball. Place the dough ball in a large, lightly oiled bowl; cover with a clean cloth and allow the dough to rise until doubled in size, about 1 hour.

4   Return the dough to the counter and reform into a ball. Cover with a towel.

5   Prepare the grill for indirect high heat (450° to 550°F). Preheat the pizza stone over indirect heat for at least 15 minutes.

6   Cut the dough ball in half and work each half into a circle measuring approximately 8 inches in diameter, with either a rolling pin or your hands.

7   Score the dough with a fork.

8   Sprinkle cornmeal on the countertop. Place the pizzas on the cornmeal and top each with sauce, sauerkraut, kielbasa, and cheese.

9   Sprinkle more cornmeal on the peel and transfer the first pizza from the countertop to the pizza stone.

10   Grill the pizza with the lid down for 5 to 7 minutes or until the dough is cooked. Repeat with the second pizza.

GRILLED CHICKEN, SHALLOT, AND
ARUGULA PIZZA

★ **SERVES 2**

★ **INGREDIENTS**

FOR THE SAUCE

2 tablespoons unsalted butter

2 tablespoons all-purpose flour

1 cup milk

6 fresh basil leaves, chopped

1 clove garlic, minced

½ cup Parmigiano-Reggiano cheese, grated

⅛ teaspoon kosher salt

FOR THE PIZZA

Pre-made pizza dough

1 cup chopped grilled chicken

¼ cup Parmigiano-Reggiano cheese, grated

¼ cup low-moisture mozzarella cheese, shredded

1 shallot, thinly sliced

½ cup arugula

★ **EQUIPMENT**

Wax paper

★ **BEER PAIRING**

Red Ale

A lot of meals I grill start from scratch, especially pizza. While it may seem daunting, dough-making is easy, and the taste of homemade dough is amazing and worth the extra effort. However, sometimes life intervenes and I decide to make pizza at the last minute. When I'm in a hurry, store-bought, pre-made pizza dough—whether fresh or frozen—works great, so I've featured it here. Not to throw another curveball, but I've also included a white sauce in this recipe instead of the traditional tomato sauce. Fun fact: Some of my favorite pizzas do not have tomato sauce. I consider this one of them!

1 In a small skillet over medium heat, melt the butter. Add the flour to the butter and whisk constantly until combined and fragrant, about 1 minute.

2 Raise the temperature of the skillet to medium high and slowly add the milk while whisking. Add the basil and garlic. Continue to whisk until the sauce thickens and coats the back of a spoon, about 3 to 4 minutes.

3 Reduce the heat to low. Stir in the parmesan until the cheese melts. Stir in salt.

4 Prepare the grill for indirect medium-high heat (400° to 450°F).

5 Roll out the dough and place it onto wax paper. Lightly brush each side with olive oil. Score the dough with a fork.

6 Grill the pizza dough over direct heat until the dough begins to set up and is marked by the grill, approximately 1 to 2 minutes.

7 Return the pizza dough to the wax paper, grilled-side up.

8 Top with the sauce, chicken, cheeses, shallot, and arugula.

9 Grill the pizza over indirect heat with the lid down for 5 to 6 minutes or until the dough is cooked.

⫸ INDEX ⫷